PHIL GELDART

EXPERIENTIAL LEARNING

CHANGING BEHAVIOR TO IMPROVE PERFORMANCE

ISBN 9780993936043

Dedication

To Sabrina, Stefan, Sean, and Rebekah for their unwavering support on our own lifelong experiential learning journey.

With particular thanks to Jenny Schmidt for her incredibly talented contribution to the look and feel of our programs, and this book.

"Let us not become weary in doing good,
for at the proper time we will reap a harvest if we do not give up."
– Galatians 6:9

TABLE OF CONTENTS

Forward

1. How It All Started...

13. Why Experiential Learning Works

39. Themes

49. "But I Don't Like Games!"

57. The Debrief

79. A Case Study in How to Create an Experience

96. The Adventure Continues...

98. Appendix – Additional Resources on Experiential Learning

FORWARD

Since Eagle's Flight first brought experiential learning to the training and development world in 1989, there has been an ever-increasing appreciation for its effectiveness as a behavior change tool. With that appreciation has also come much greater demand for it to be part of training curriculum designs.

However, considerable confusion has also arisen about just what actually constitutes effective experiential learning. Is it a simulation? An engaging activity? An outdoors rope course? Just fun? A business game? And why is it really so powerful?

As with any new idea taking root, considerable confusion can exist about the nature of this new thinking. A wide variety of offerings, each with varying degrees of effectiveness, is surfacing.

There's no question that experiential learning is a powerful arrow to have in the quiver of any organization truly committed to changing human behavior, and to doing so in as cost-effective a manner as possible.

In this book I've sought to provide clarity on what experiential learning really is (or should be), why it's so powerful, and how to harness that power in any initiative or program designed to improve performance.

Also provided at the end is a practical case study that lays out the steps for creating an experiential learning program. This design is based on Eagle's Flight's own expertise in creating and using experiential learning to change behavior, often doing so through programs that have been customized, or uniquely created, to meet specific client needs.

I trust that you'll be energized by what you see and read, and that this will serve to bring clarity, and define a standard, for those incorporating this tool into their own programs, and so truly shaping the future of training.

Phil Geldart

HOW IT ALL STARTED…

Experiential Learning *brings to life things not so readily seen…*

In this picture the "camels" are really shadows. The actual camels are the small white "lines" at the feet of each "camel."

HOW IT ALL STARTED…

In the early '80s, I had just been given responsibility for training at Nestlé Canada. It was a new position for them, as there had been little by way of a "training department" before that...and now I was the department!

At that time I was relatively young, from Head Office, leading a function that had yet to prove itself. I had a great boss who encouraged me to take the necessary time to put together a strong program, and gave me the freedom to figure out what that should be. I did just that, and after several months was ready to go.

I'd created a yearlong curriculum for various levels within the company, and the first one to be delivered was to be Time Management for Managers. The way the schedule was set up, it happened that my first session was to be at one of our factories, about 100 miles from Head Office.

I was ready to go.

As I was reviewing my material in preparation for my first ever stand-up training delivery, a day or so in advance, I thought about what was to happen...these seasoned managers at a world-class facility were about to be asked to attend a course on time management. Further, the course was to be taught by a junior employee, from Head Office, who'd never worked in a factory in his life!

I had done my homework and felt that the content of the course was very strong and would benefit them; but on reflection, I felt that my chances of being accepted, and really given an open mind by the intended participants, were exceptionally low. If I'd been in their position, I think I might well have been asking if this corporate trainer could really add any significant value to me and my job.

I suspected that my professional career as a trainer was about to come to an abrupt end!

But the content was good, I thought. So...how to get them to realize that it would be worthwhile to stick with me for the day, and how to make the learnings really personal, visceral, and relevant?

From that sense of mild panic – that if I didn't do something dramatic my success rate was probably going to be dismal – came the idea to embed the learning into a game. Not just any game, but one that would both show them that they could get better, and then how to be better.

The more I thought about this approach the better it seemed. If they were to play a game, then they'd be bringing their own skills and abilities to it. It wouldn't be a "role-play," which I knew everyone saw as "not real"; and it wouldn't be a case study, which would seem theoretical. It would be them being themselves, acting as they normally would, and getting the result that fully reflected their own abilities.

SO...HOW TO DESIGN THE GAME?

▶ *Coke and barbecue chips have become synonymous with creativity at Eagle's Flight...as they're my own go-to "brain food" when creating a new experience.*

"If they were to play a game, then they'd be bringing their own skills and abilities to it."

Since it was about optimizing performance (the real objective behind time management), and the power of really effective planning (key to great results), the idea of a performance-based adventure seemed appropriate. By adding in the opportunity to plan at the beginning, and making that a crucial component of success, the game would reflect what I wanted to teach during the day.

To add some intensity and real-life relevance, I felt that it should be competitive in some way...so putting the participants in small teams competing with each other seemed to accomplish that. Plus, working as teams not only reflected how they actually worked, but would also provide some personal safety, in that no one individual would be singled out at the end when the results were announced.

These were factory people who were very focused on results and the metrics that tracked those results, so I felt that there had to be an objective, undebatable way to measure their performance. The winning team would be the one with the best score, but very importantly, there would be an optimal score.

This I thought was key. If they were to learn anything, there had to be a best way to play the game, a best way to perform. If they followed certain principles, then they would optimize their game performance, and these principles would be the same ones I was about to teach in the course. Following these principles on the job would result in optimum performance there too.

So...to work! I didn't have a lot of time to create this game, since my first session was just around the corner.

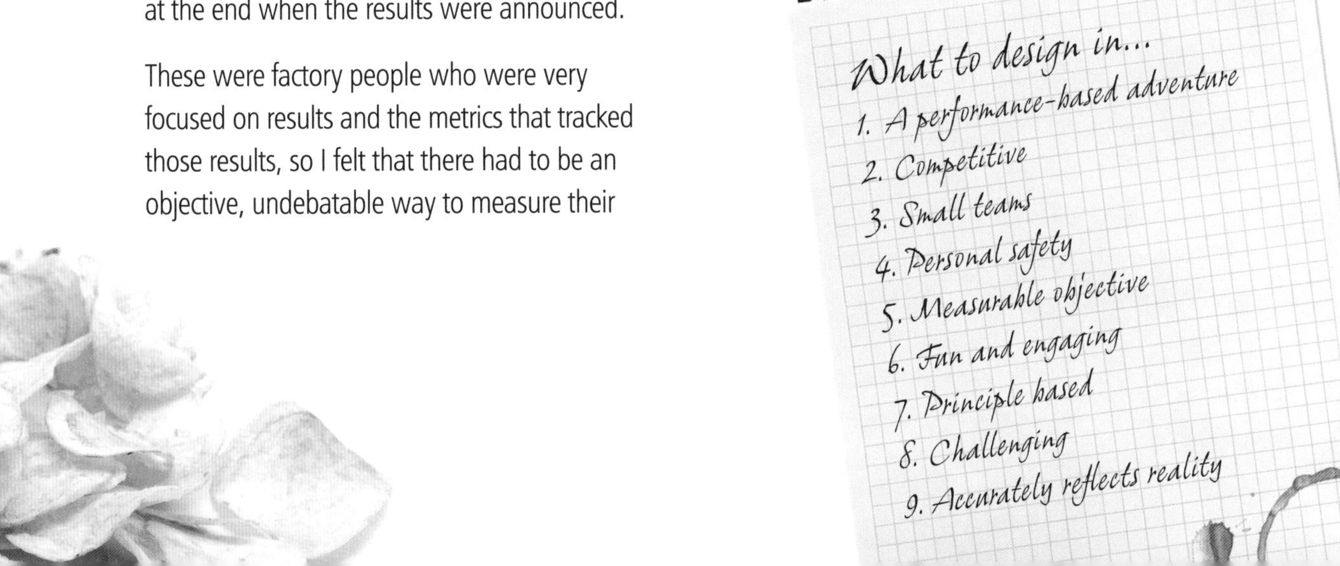

I decided on a desert theme because of the need to plan up front before heading out into the desert (where food and water would be needed every day). It seemed reasonable to have a starting point where they could plan and get supplies before venturing out…home base.

In life there are always options available, and a need to cope with the unforeseen, but there are also ways to deal with these variables. In fact, much of the training was to be around optimizing in the face of the unforeseen, and learning how best to select the options that would yield both the greatest chance of success, and the best possible result.

This thinking led to adding components to the game like oases and the mysterious Tomb of Kings in the desert, as well as somewhat unpredictable weather patterns that they would encounter once underway. Options to cope with these uncertainties would be available at home base, if they wished to take advantage of them.

I also felt that available information used effectively was a key component of optimizing productivity, so I added that element to the game. They would have the option of getting valuable information at home base, but at a cost. I felt that most people recognize the value of useful information in theory, but are often unwilling to take the time necessary to get and then digest it. They would rather "figure things out along the way," and get on with the task. So, I made information available, but apparently costly.

The last step was to create a crystal clear objective. Gold always seems popular as a goal for adventurers, so I made gold available in the distant mountains. To be successful, they would have to cross a vast and perilous desert, moving at a rate of once per day. Their goal was to get to the mountains, mine for gold as many days as possible, then return with their gold to home base, after once again surviving the dangerous return journey across the desert.

I'd give them 25 game days to complete the adventure, and make each day last three minutes so they could adapt and adjust as they went.

That was the plan that I hoped would set this day of training apart for them, and set me up for success. I'd run the game first thing, and then, hopefully, have their attention for the rest of the day, as I showed them how the game was really just a metaphor for their day-to-day work. By applying the principles that would allow them to win in the game back on the job, they would be far more productive after the training.

*"I decided on a **desert theme** because of the need for considerable up-front planning before heading out into any desert."*

I pulled out a piece of flip-chart paper, and drew a desert map. Several 3x5 cards served to represent water, gold, food, and the other things I needed. Some pushpins to represent teams as they made their way across the desert, and I was ready (I hoped) to go!

"Gold of the Desert Kings™" was born.

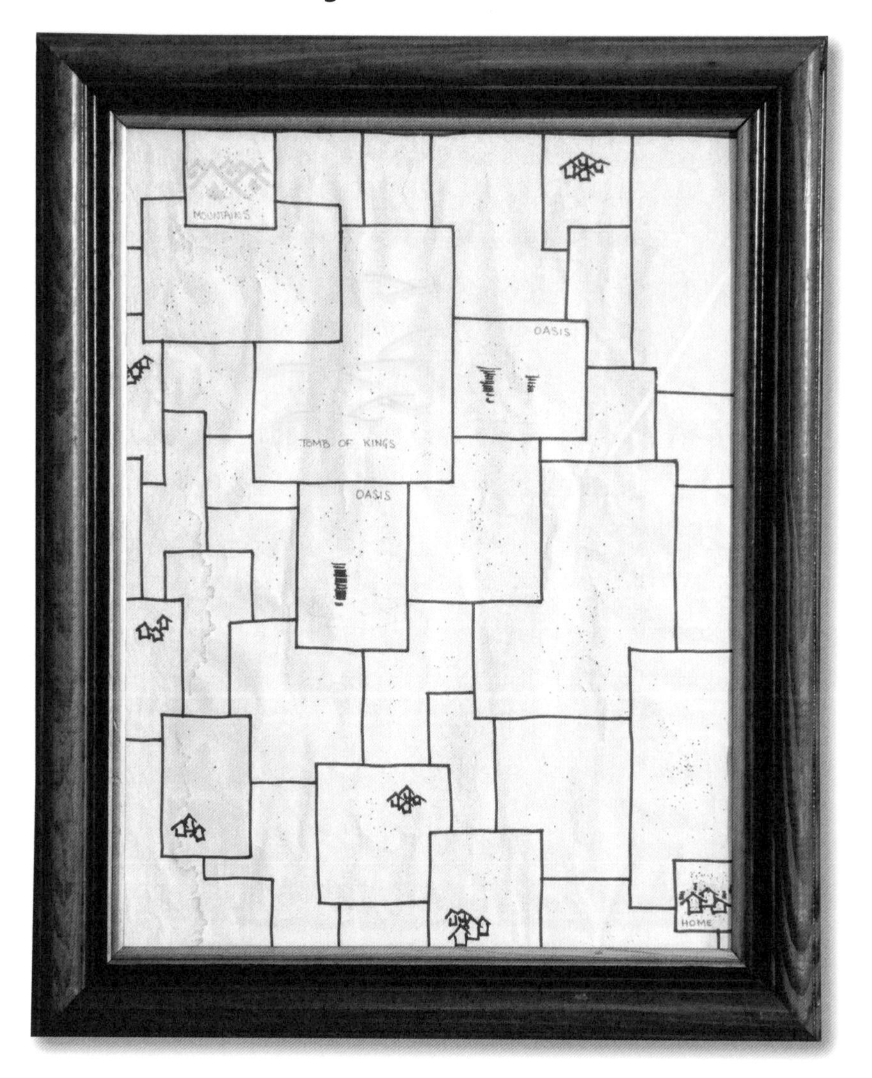

Gold of the Desert Kings™

◀ *The original map of Gold of the Desert Kings, drawn and used in my first corporate training session in 1981, is now part of Eagle's Flight folklore.*

The next morning began as I'd feared. There was little appetite in the room for a "time management course from an unseasoned corporate trainer." I acknowledged this and offered them a deal.

"You really don't want to be here for the whole day with me. I understand that. So, commit to playing a game with me for two hours. If at the end of the game you want me to stay, I will. If not, I'll pack up and you get the rest of the day free. Deal?"

Needless to say, they readily agreed.

"Okay," I said. "One question first. How many of you feel you're really good at optimizing your performance?"

Every hand shot up.

We were off. I put them in small teams, explained the rules, and let them loose.

There was not much planning, just a tremendous desire to get going. Not much time spent using the available information. Not much thought given to what would define success. Lots of energy expended, commitment to the task, working with teammates, and figuring out as they went.

They were fully engaged, and had a great time.

At the end we tallied up the scores. About 30% of the teams had embarrassingly died in the desert from lack of food or water, 40% just made it back with a little gold, and the remainder did okay, but far below what was possible. They had come back with between 4 and 6 bars of gold, when 10 were possible.

Clearly none had come close to optimizing!

*Since 1996, over 500,000 people have experienced **Gold of the Desert Kings**.*

◀ *To this day, 20% of teams still fail to plan adequately and so die in the desert.*

I then repeated the earlier question. "How good do you think you are, really, at optimizing your performance?" There was an embarrassed response as they admitted they probably weren't as good as they had thought.

I then asked how they'd feel if I debriefed the game, and showed them how to not only win in the game, but then learn to apply those same principles to perform dramatically better at work. To their credit, they enthusiastically wanted to learn more.

The day ended as a success. I kept my job, and in fact went on to become good friends with a very talented team of leaders and managers at that site.

The interesting thing was that none could claim their performance wasn't "real" in the game, because they had in truth approached it exactly as they would have any work-related issue. In reality, they were "playing" the same game every day; it was just that they were doing so over an extended period of time, so couldn't see the immediate cause and effect of their decisions and actions. These were more easily seen and reflected in a time-compressed game.

The real power came not from playing the game, but from the debrief as I was able to show them the consequences of the behaviors they had demonstrated. Had they brought different behaviors to bear, they would have experienced different and more productive consequences. These new behaviors were immediately transferable to work, and hence to improved productivity.

Experiential learning was born for me, and became a staple of all my training programs thereafter.

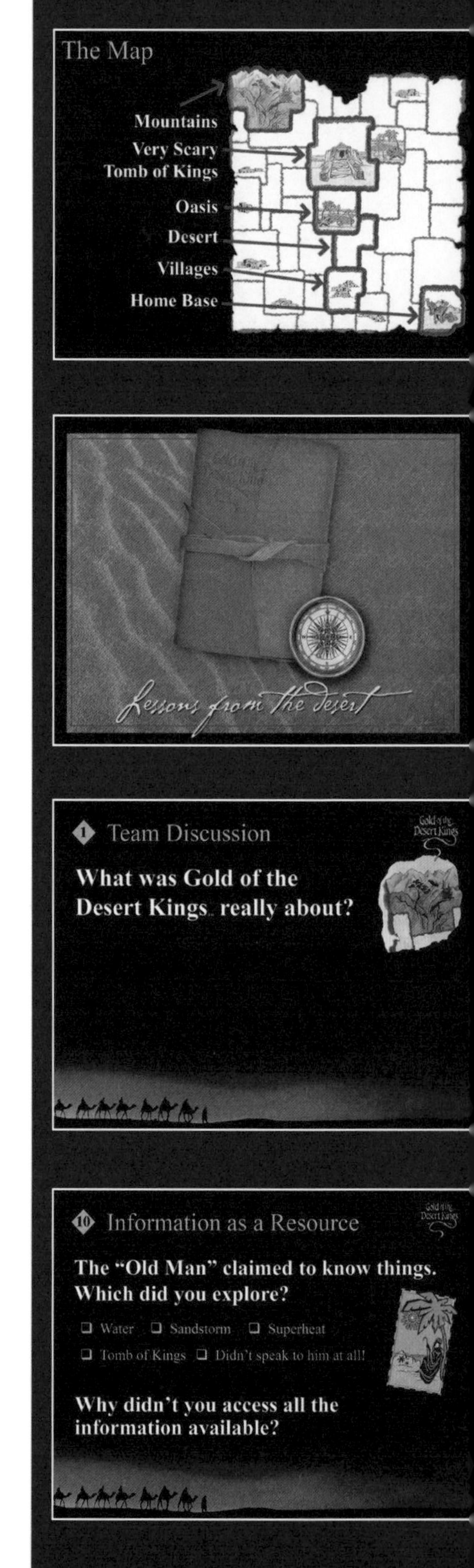

*"**Experiential learning** was born for me, and became a staple of all my training programs thereafter."*

▲ *A poster from the Training Transfer series.*

▶ *In Search of the Gold of the Desert Kings, a book written by Phil Geldart.*

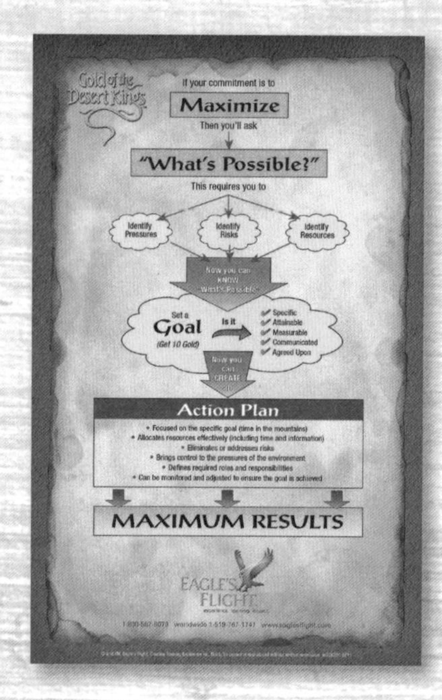

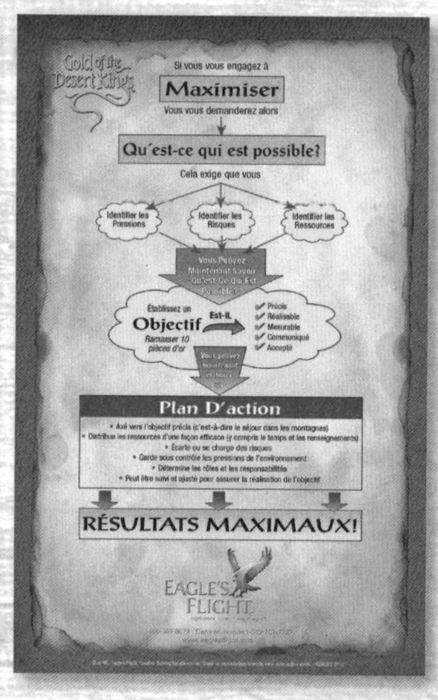

▲ *Gold of the Desert Kings has been translated into over 24 languages worldwide.*

▼ *Post-training retention email series helps to keep key learnings top of mind.*

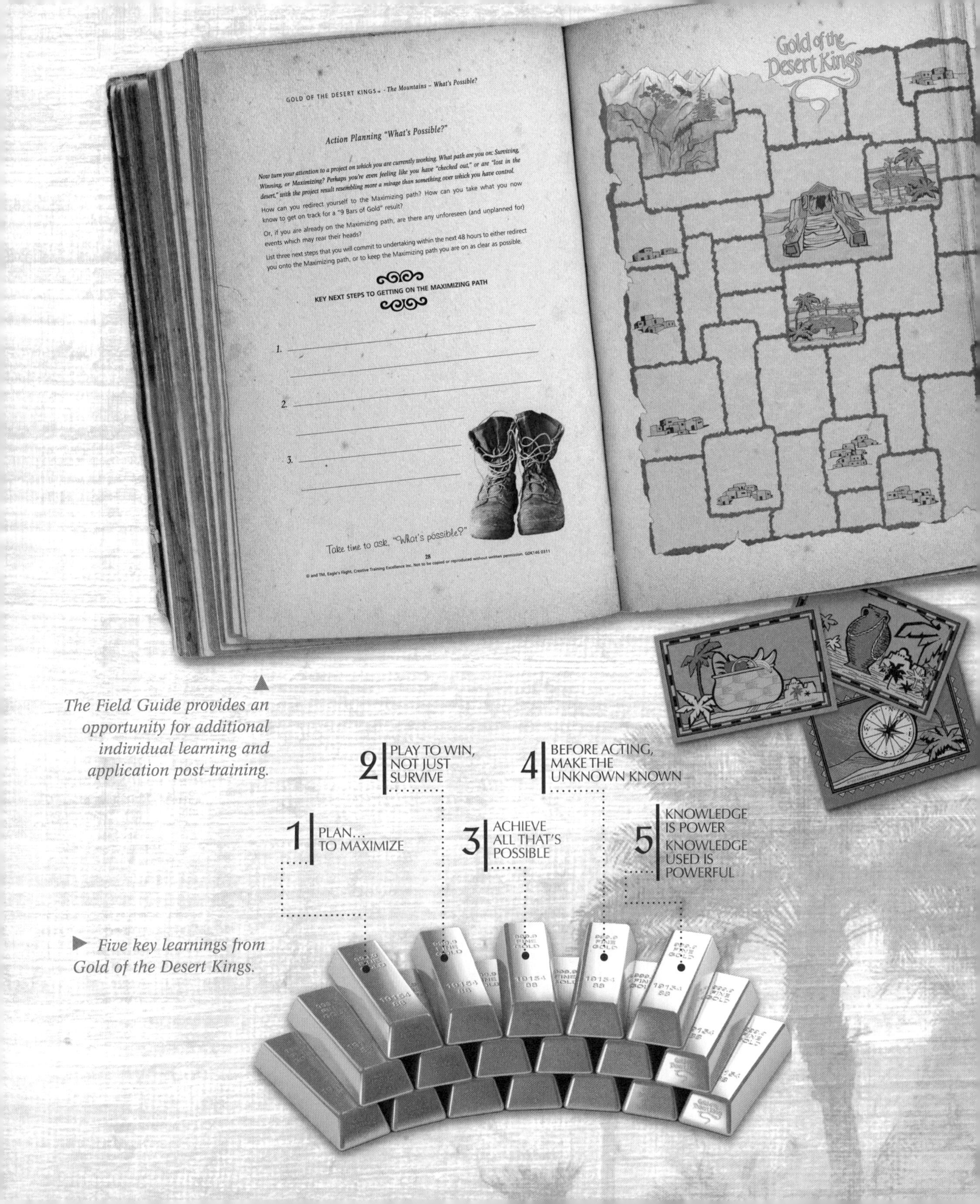

The Field Guide provides an opportunity for additional individual learning and application post-training.

Five key learnings from Gold of the Desert Kings.

WHY EXPERIENTIAL LEARNING WORKS

The objective of company-provided training, and in fact most training of any kind, is to improve performance, and hence results, in some way.

THE STANDARD TRAINING APPROACH

To meet the objectives stated above, the primary vehicle is knowledge transfer. Information is transmitted to the participants in some way...via a trainer, or with PowerPoints, or video, or some form of digital delivery. This form of learning is valuable to some degree, but limited. There are many factors working against it being a success.

- People tend to remember only a fraction of what they hear
- It can easily become difficult to pay attention to (i.e., it becomes repetitive or boring)
- We tend to learn best by doing, not listening
- The content itself may be uninteresting
- The participant may often feel that they don't need, or want, the learning
- The person presenting may be a subject matter expert, but not equally skilled in delivery
- There is no personal conviction demonstrated on the part of the presenter that motivates the participant to really want to internalize and apply the information
- Simply being given information in no way guarantees that the participant truly understands that content

STANDARD TRAINING OPTIONS

To attempt to compensate for these shortfalls, a number of options are available. Each of these approaches brings strength to the learning that occurs from the dissemination of information, and facilitates that learning. They each also have significant drawbacks.

1

Role-play scenarios can be introduced, allowing participants to practice the new learning. These have a place, primarily where the learning is expected to be applied in predictable scenarios; for example, presenting the benefits of a new product, or learning to teach others how to do something.

DRAWBACK

The role-plays are not "real," in that participants must "pretend" to be in the situation, or to be someone they're not, or use skills that are not yet familiar to them.

2

Case-study work is an excellent way for the participants to mentally "chew over" the information provided in an effort to make it their own, and to better understand it. Case-study work can also be used to provide a discussion on how the information could be applied in theory. This last point is important to note, in that case-study discussions are by definition theoretical. They add to knowledge and understanding, but not to real-world application.

DRAWBACK

The conclusions from case-study discussions may not actually apply when brought into the actual work environment because of factors that were not foreseen or included.

3

There are multiple **digital tools** available to help with application. These are essentially decision-tree scenarios, or turn-based situations, where participants are offered choices, and based on the learning have an opportunity to decide on a course of action. The "correct" choice allows the participant to advance; the "incorrect" choice requires that they try again.

DRAWBACK

The digital practice approach can be seen as too linear, not allowing for the natural environment of the workplace where things are often not as straightforward or simple as they appear in the practice work.

Digital tools are particularly powerful when there is in fact a correct answer (for example, the correct way to operate a deep fryer). They are less valuable when there is no "correct" answer, but rather a need for judgment (for example, in handling a difficult coaching situation).

They are also excellent when used post-course to reinforce what was taught, and practiced, in the course itself.

4

Exercises and activities are also used to illustrate some aspect of the content, or to allow participants to practice what they just heard.

DRAWBACK

The exercises or activities, unless very well crafted, often do not allow the participants to include their own knowledge and experience base, or take reasonable personal initiative to achieve the best possible outcome.

Exercises and activities can be very powerful, when the participants are given a situation that is actually drawn from their day-to-day work, and then asked to apply the new learning to that situation with the objective of achieving a better outcome than they could have before the learning. The key here is to ensure that the real-life work situation is accurately portrayed, and the activity carefully designed to allow for application of the specific new learning.

THE EXPERIENTIAL LEARNING APPROACH

Experiential learning is not by itself the only way to deliver training. However, when included with the other forms of training just identified, it will optimize the potential impact of that training.

Experiential learning can be the difference between actually changing behavior, and only providing more information, with limited real behavior change.

There are eight key reasons for this.

1. A powerful experience will immerse the participants in the same way that real-world challenges do. Participants are fully engaged, and committed to achieving an outcome with the same passion and intensity that is displayed at work. It very quickly loses any sense of being a "training exercise," and rapidly becomes totally immersive. The real person brings their real skills to bear on a real situation.
2. The experience is not seen as simply a simulation of their real world. Rather, the activity is deliberately themed to mask any connection to their day-to-day reality. They must bring their capabilities to bear on what appears to be a totally different challenge than they usually face, in an environment that is unique; for example, building a bridge between two islands to save the indigenous turtle population.

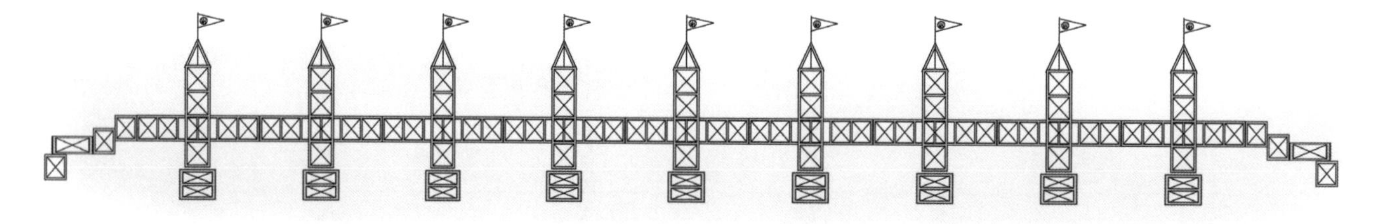

3. It's typically captivating, and fun. I've seen participants begin the experience with a stated intention of "not participating," or worse, the unstated intention of simply withdrawing. Typically, it's not very long before each of these people is drawn into the experience by the storyline, and the challenge that their team faces. They quickly become fully engaged along with the rest.

4. The experience is an exact metaphor for the reality faced by the participants, and hence the debrief is powerful, relevant, and engaging. Participants want to know what they can learn from the experience, and how that learning would have helped them to succeed. As they realize how exact a metaphor it was to their real world, they quickly see the parallels. They realize how they can improve performance on the job by applying the lessons learned in the debrief. (Clearly, the experience used in the course to teach a particular topic must be an appropriate match.)

5. The results obtained in the experience are the results of behavior demonstrated during the experience by the team, and the individuals on that team. This is an undisputed reality. Once participants see that connection clearly, it is an easy step to show them new behaviors, and to make the link to improved results. Those improved results will come whenever the new behaviors are applied, regardless of the situation. The results will improve whether the behaviors are applied at work, at home, or in one's personal life.

▲ *In Coral Banks, building a bridge to save turtles puts focus on teamwork and optimizing team productivity.*

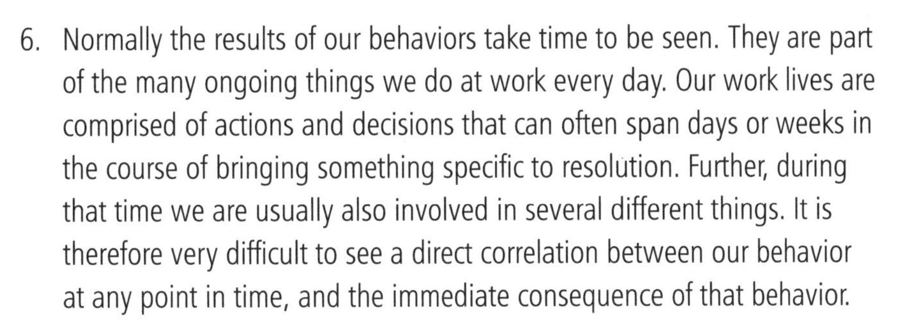

6. Normally the results of our behaviors take time to be seen. They are part of the many ongoing things we do at work every day. Our work lives are comprised of actions and decisions that can often span days or weeks in the course of bringing something specific to resolution. Further, during that time we are usually also involved in several different things. It is therefore very difficult to see a direct correlation between our behavior at any point in time, and the immediate consequence of that behavior.

In an experience, time is compressed into an hour or two at most. Further, there is intense focus on a single desired outcome (although often a complicated one).

This then allows for demonstration of a clear line of sight between cause (behavior) and effect (result). It is this time compression that makes the learning brought out in the debrief so powerful and personal.

7. Because the experience itself is heavily themed, and usually not related to a specific business problem, it allows for great flexibility in the debrief. Typically the experience will bring principles to life that are relevant to the content being trained; in the debrief, the facilitator can then choose which principle to concentrate on, and how much time to give to each. This flexibility allows for maximum on-the-job relevance to be made.

8. One of the greatest hurdles faced in any training is that of building conviction in the participants that they need to change, and then that they actually can change. After having completed an experience, participants have fully participated in something concrete, and have clearly seen the result – usually one that is well below their expectation and desired outcome. After the debrief they understand why, and what to do going forward to change that result. Because this is something they've now personally experienced, and viscerally understood, they develop a deep-seated personal conviction about the value of changing, and the approach to take to be more successful going forward.

One Potential Risk

The only real potential risk to experiential learning is not having a highly relevant debrief. Without this, the participants will see only a game and no rationale for its inclusion in the course; or they may feel it was good, but not worth the time. Without the ability to clearly link the experience to improving on-the-job performance, the power of experiential learning will be completely lost.

Versatility

When experiential learning is included with more classical training approaches, it's easy to see why that training day is so much more effective.

Depending on the desired outcome, it's often possible to simply run a powerful experience followed by a carefully crafted debrief, and so have a profound impact on behavior without additional training. In that case, the debrief must be extremely relevant to the on-the-job reality, and be reinforced for some time afterwards to keep the new learnings top of mind.

"Representations of K'NEX pieces and their use herein is with the express permission of K'NEX Industries, Inc. Hatfield, PA"

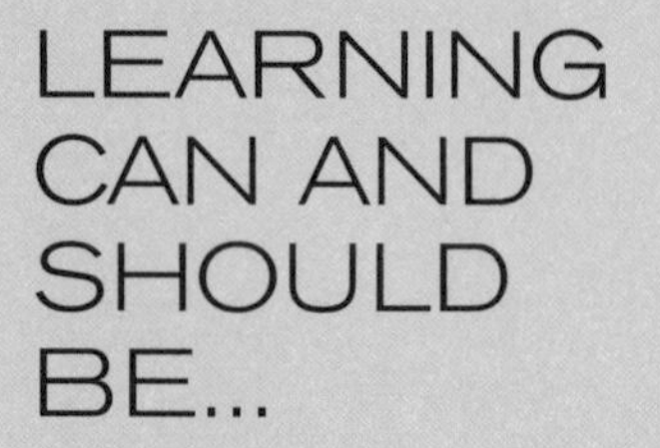

LEARNING CAN AND SHOULD BE... FUN!

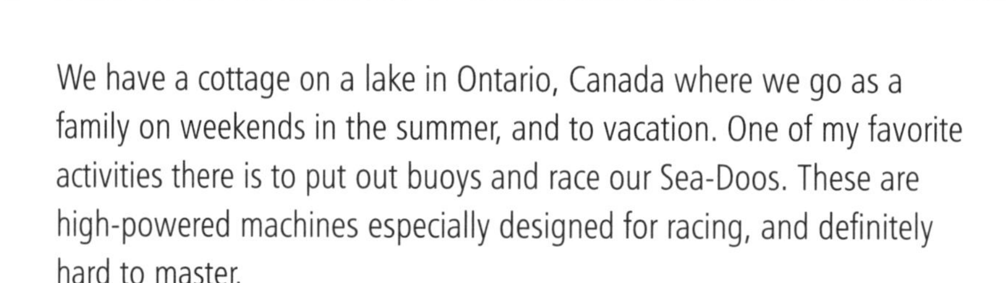

We have a cottage on a lake in Ontario, Canada where we go as a family on weekends in the summer, and to vacation. One of my favorite activities there is to put out buoys and race our Sea-Doos. These are high-powered machines especially designed for racing, and definitely hard to master.

We frequently take the machines out and compete, constantly trying to better our own time around the course, and also that of our friendly competitors. We share race tips, ways we've discovered to shave off a few seconds, and techniques we're working on that improve performance.

This is serious fun!

Learning to get better, and then applying that learning on the next run through the course, only makes the time on the water that much more enjoyable.

I share this because somehow we often feel that "fun" and "learning" need to be mutually exclusive...that is, corporate training shouldn't be fun, and certainly not enjoyable. I don't agree with that viewpoint at all.

Tongo's TOWER™

Learning to be better on the Sea-Doos is fun in itself. This very fact – that learning to improve is fun – provides additional motivation to work at getting better. If it weren't fun, then I think we'd be far less willing to go out on the water and continually try to increase our skill, and our understanding of what's required to deliver increasingly better lap times. The fact that the learning itself is fun, and that the resulting improvement is so rewarding, makes the time on the Sea-Doos great.

"This very fact – that learning to improve is fun – provides additional motivation to work at getting better."

When we think about providing training at work with the express intention of improving performance, adding a component that actually makes the learning fun should be a priority. Doing so increases the interest level for the participants, increases their degree of engagement, and I believe also accelerates their learning, in that it encourages people to bring more of themselves to the process.

Experiential learning then becomes even more important, as it is perhaps the most effective way to bring relevant fun into the training environment.

▲ *Learning to perform better through personal experience and input received can definitely be fun!*

WE REMEMBER WHAT WE DO FAR MORE THAN WHAT WE HEAR

The objective of any training is ultimately to change behavior. For that to happen, there are four elements that must be included.

The individual must want to change.

There must be some conviction on the part of the learner that changing would be beneficial, or required, or worth pursuing. Without this desire to change on the part of the learner, any teaching or training provided will be in vain...there's no intrinsic motivation to remember or apply it, so it will essentially be lost.

Knowledge must be transmitted.

Information must be transferred from the one teaching to the ones learning. For all intents and purposes, this is purely an intellectual activity. The goal is to inform on how or why to do something. It is at this step that participants develop an intellectual understanding of the new behaviors and, usually, how they differ from the behaviors participants currently have, or don't have but need.

This information must move from theoretical to practical.

How to implement what was just taught needs to be made clear, as well as how to do so within the context of the participants' day-to-day responsibilities. At this step the learning must shift from information to competence. Those being taught will need to know the steps to follow to use the training: how to overcome hurdles, how to deal with the unexpected, and how to develop confidence in their ability to use the new information received in practice.

There must be some improved results from the application of the learning.

It's one thing to know how to do something or behave differently, but it's quite another to use those new skills "in the heat of the battle." There are many things working against the application of new behaviors: old habits, time pressure, peer pressure, lack of support from a supervisor, lack of personal confidence, and just plain forgetting what was learned. Yet without the results expected from the training occurring on the job, the first three steps are useless, no matter how well done.

FIRE kindles FIRE...
CONVICTION not only changes individual BEHAVIOR, but is also CONTAGIOUS!

HEART
Build conviction

There is usually very little effort put into building or enhancing conviction. The assumption is that participants will have to deal with that on their own, that is, "It's what they should bring to the party." I think this is the wrong way to think about it. Very often participants aren't motivated to learn, or lack conviction to change, not because they are malicious in some way, but rather because they just don't see the value – yet – of the training, or more likely, they don't know that there is value there to be had. This was the situation with the story I told in the first chapter about the birth of experiential learning.

We need to be careful not to ignore the need to build conviction. In fact, I would suggest that without addressing this as the first step, what follows may be of little long-term value. And conversely, putting meaningful thought and effort into this first step will serve to multiply the impact of all the training that follows.

People generally remember only about **10%** of what they **HEAR**

HEAD
Provide knowledge

Information is usually presented in a combination of lecture and PowerPoint or video. Because this is the least effective way for people to learn, instructors need to be very careful how many content topics they present in a single session, and how much information they try to convey for each topic. People generally remember only about 10% of what they hear and understand. If they don't understand it in the first place, that low retention rate will drop even lower.

Adding images (pictures, charts, and illustrations) will help greatly, as the human mind tends to store pictures much better than words for recall. Using video can further enhance the delivery impact.

However, regardless of the presenter's skill, and the careful crafting of the content, delivery, and materials, by itself this is still a very poor way to pass on information. As humans, we remember much more when we do than when we hear. If we can learn by doing, by experimentation, by trial and error, by cause and effect, by being personally and actively involved, then we learn better, more quickly, and more permanently than we do by passive listening.

A highly talented individual was once asked how he became so competent, that is, what led to his success. His answer was: "Good decisions." When asked how he developed that ability to make good decisions, he responded: "Experience." When he was then queried about how he gained this experience, he replied: "Bad decisions."

This is a great illustration of the power of learning by doing, rather than by listening. Clearly not all training can avoid lecture, PowerPoint, and explanation. All learning must include that to some degree. The point is to recognize the very significant limitations of these tools and attempt to mitigate their shortcomings with more opportunities to include learning by doing.

HANDS
Teach skills

When it comes to practice and helping participants apply the information presented, there must be a "do" component, almost by definition. However, as with "Heart" (conviction), adequate time is often not spent on this. Instead, more time than ever is given to theory, that is, more information presented, more PowerPoint slides, more videos. Often the "Hands" component is ostensibly addressed using case-study work. Unfortunately, this is still information, perspective, and theory.

If there is effort expended in this area, it is typically far too little to have the impact required to truly change behavior. At Eagle's Flight, we frequently use our "40, 40, 20" formula. This translates to 40% of the time spent on conviction and knowledge transfer, 40% on practice with that knowledge, and then 20% on the post-course application of the learning to generate the expected impact from changed behavior. There is clearly some overlap in each of these buckets, and also the need to consider the appropriate mix for each specific outcome.

The point here is that far more time needs to be spent on the "Hands" portion – the practice. This is working with the content under the guidance of the instructor until there's mastery of the new behaviors.

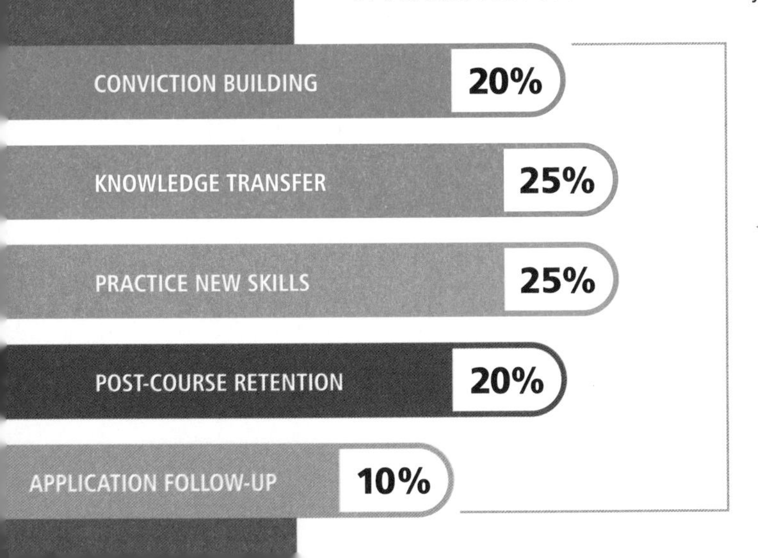

This is a guideline for optimal training impact.

HARVEST
See results

This is the post-class activity that follows any training, and it is vital to seeing long-lasting, sustained behavior change. Again, training initiatives often overlook providing adequate focus on this area.

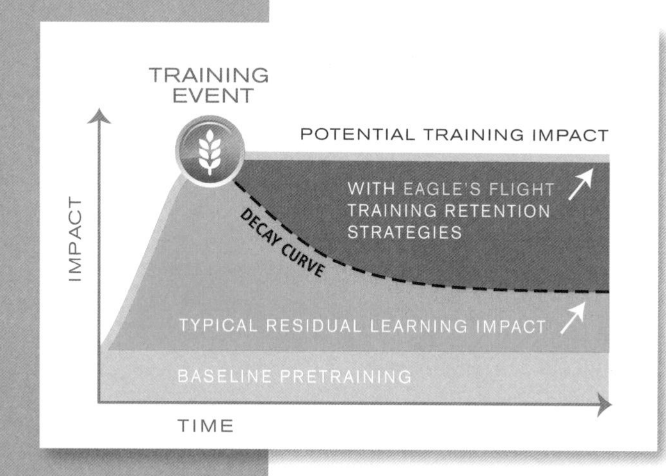

▲ *Measurement and post-class retention minimize the decay curve and maximize the training impact.*

There is much that should be considered here. However, a key component is enlisting the participants' leaders in the process, so they can encourage, coach, and commend the expected new behaviors as they begin to be demonstrated on the job.

Small group "application discussions" that last 60-90 minutes, and occur every three weeks or so with other participants, are also very effective. Ideally, these are facilitated either by the original instructor, or another leader with personal mastery of the content. Their purpose is for the participants to be able to talk with their colleagues about the successes and challenges they're having with the application of the new content.

Digital gamification and retention tools can also be very effective, and reasonably economical to deploy.

Clearly there must also be tracking of the improved results that are coming from the retention and application of these new behaviors, and made a priority in order to overtly draw a line of sight between the new behaviors and those improved results. This is another area where the participants' leaders can add great value.

There are several other approaches that can be taken, but the primary principle is to ensure that the "Harvest" component receives considerable thought and attention.

THE POTENTIAL FOR EXPERIENTIAL LEARNING TO IMPACT HEART, HEAD, HANDS, AND HARVEST

Experiential learning can play a significant and very powerful role in each of these four areas, and therefore should be considered at each stage.

Conviction occurs when an individual has come to the personal realization that there is benefit from adopting a different course of action than they would normally pursue. From that they will look to determine what they can do differently and then how to do it.

After completing an experience, the participants have a chance to reflect on what just happened and why. With the help of the post-experience debrief, they come to personally see the link between their actions and their results, and also have the opportunity to examine alternatives that could have been chosen. From that, they can draw their own conclusions about the power of mastering new approaches and behaviors.

These realizations are very powerful in that they come as a result of conclusions drawn by the participants themselves. They are not something that has been simply explained; rather, they have been discovered. They have become personal as a result of what each participant did and experienced. This conviction, which has come from participating in the experience, now "prepares the soil for the seed," reinforcing the value of developing the new skills and behaviors that will come from absorbing the information that will follow.

◀ *Council of the Marble Star builds conviction around the importance of getting results, and demonstrating corporate values, both having to coexist.*

Typically experiential learning is not used as much for the "Head" component of training, lending itself more to "Heart" and "Hands." However, this is not always the case. **Eagle's Flight has an intriguing program called Lord Devon's Demise™ which in fact provides both the content (head) and the practice (hands) in one experience.**

The topic that this program covers is Meetings Management, an often overlooked area where few have real mastery, yet which is a critical skill. Meetings are a vital part of virtually all sales calls, figure into effective management capabilities, and are part of both innovation and continuous process improvement activities – and these are just a few instances where skillful meetings management is key to improving performance.

In Lord Devon's Demise, participants enter the room and are immediately seated in groups of five or six. They are then told that they are Inspectors at Scotland Yard. It's the era of Agatha Christie, and Lord Devon has recently been found murdered at his estate after hosting a weekend party there.

Participants are to work in the groups to which they've been assigned, and will have six days in which to solve the murder before the Chief Inspector arrives expecting the crime to be solved. Time will pass so quickly that each day will seem like a mere 20 minutes!

◀ *Lord Devon's Demise is an experience that teaches how to lead effective meetings.*

It is based on a murder-mystery plot set in the early 1920s, and the era of Agatha Christie.

▲ *During the investigation, a series of clues are handed out. They need to be unraveled in a series of meetings held at Scotland Yard.*

They're given all the evidence found so far – a cocktail napkin, a chess pawn, interview statements taken by the constable initially called, and the murder weapon (Lord Devon's letter opener), among other things.

After Day 1, participants are overwhelmed, and the facilitator asks if they'd like a tool to help them with the challenge before them. The answer is always yes, at which point the facilitator shares a seven-step approach, and explains how to use it going forward.

Day 2 begins...with yet more evidence, and notification that more criminal activity occurred over the weekend at the estate than just murder!

After each "day," the facilitator debriefs how well they're using the seven-step tool, what they could be doing to improve their skill with it, and asks which step they will concentrate on during the next "day" to optimize their group's performance.

By the time the six days are over, they've discovered that not just one, but nine crimes were committed that weekend! They've worked through forensic reports, clues, witness statements, and even discovered the part played by Fifi the dog. They've successfully solved each crime by first using, and then mastering, the use of the seven-step tool, and can now each run an effective and highly productive meeting.

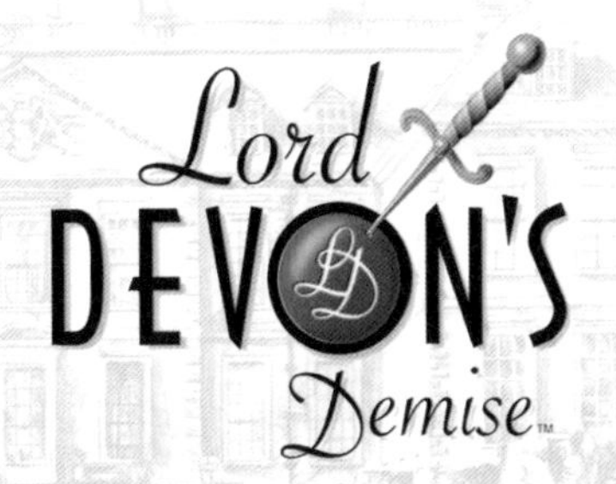

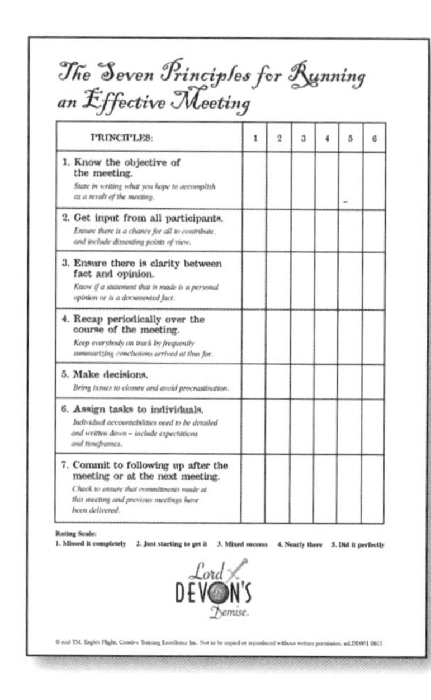

The Seven Principles for Running an Effective Meeting

PRINCIPLES:	1	2	3	4	5	6
1. Know the objective of the meeting. *State in writing what you hope to accomplish as a result of the meeting.*						
2. Get input from all participants. *Ensure there is a chance for all to contribute, and include dissenting points of view.*						
3. Ensure there is clarity between fact and opinion. *Know if a statement that is made is a personal opinion or is a documented fact.*						
4. Recap periodically over the course of the meeting. *Keep everybody on track by frequently summarizing conclusions arrived at thus far.*						
5. Make decisions. *Bring issues to closure and avoid procrastination.*						
6. Assign tasks to individuals. *Individual accountabilities need to be detailed and written down – include expectations and timeframes.*						
7. Commit to following up after the meeting or at the next meeting. *Check to ensure that commitments made at this meeting and previous meetings have been delivered.*						

Rating Scale:
1. Missed it completely 2. Just starting to get it 3. Mixed success 4. Nearly there 5. Did it perfectly

Lord DEVON'S Demise.

This is an example of using experiential learning to both teach content and allow for repeated practice of that content until mastery. The participants have fun, don't really realize they're mastering meetings management until it's all over, and leave with confidence and capability in the application of a new behavior.

There are a number of other ways to use experiential learning to help with the practice component of skills development, whether it's something as straightforward as customer service, or in the leadership arena with something like Executional Excellence™. In each case the experience must mirror the content that was taught earlier so that the practice is relevant.

In terms of post-class reinforcement, experiential learning can be helpful in two ways. Initially it will provide a common language and set of metaphors that are readily recognized by all. This makes it very easy, and effective, to reference the content and the lessons after the training. The metaphors can be incorporated into any one of several reinforcement tools, and the language will provide a vocabulary that will help with coaching. It provides an immediately recognized understanding of what behavior is being referred to by the coach.

◄ *A series of post-training emails are used to reinforce the program's principles.*

The second opportunity is less frequently used simply because it may not be possible to reassemble the class six months or so later. However, if this is possible, then having the group work through a single experience related to their earlier learning can be very powerful, if the experience is appropriately selected.

The goal is to remind participants of the learnings, give them an opportunity to practice again under the guidance of the facilitator, and do a robust postmortem debrief of their performance. The experience should be designed to be more challenging than what they originally encountered to take the learnings deeper; or it could be used simply to reinforce conviction, and emphasize again the power of using the behaviors taught a number of months ago.

Regardless of how experiential learning is used, it can significantly add to each of the four components of any training event. Since we remember what we do far more than what we hear, incorporating experiences into training programs makes them both much more memorable, and far more effective, thereby truly adding value to the organization.

▼ *Theming is an important part of every experiential learning event. It creates the context and environment necessary to pull participants into the reality of the experience.*

THE POWER OF COMMON LANGUAGE AND EXPERIENCE

In the Eagle's Flight experience **Rattlesnake Canyon**™, teams are pitted against each other to make as much money as possible by supplying the needs of the Eagle Bend Railroad, which is building a line through Rattlesnake Canyon.

The settlers are buying basic materials like livestock, spikes, lumber, blankets, tools, lanterns, and horses from the wagon trains and steamboat suppliers. They are in turn selling these items to the merchants, who then add value by assembling items into kits for subsequent sale to the railroad.

There are literally dozens of items that combine in different ways to make up several types of kits. Once the railroad has all they require of one type of kit (e.g., a building kit of 50 picks, 30 axes, and 70 shovels), they no longer purchase those kits.

The experience is designed to teach the power of partnership (possible between settlers and merchants), and the importance of knowing and meeting the evolving needs of the customer (the railroad). There are many other principles embedded in the experience, but those are two primary ones.

Once the experience is under way, there is a tremendous amount of noise, energy, and activity as dozens of teams move to optimize their profit. There are four "weeks" in the game (each about 20 minutes long) and each year brings new challenges and a shifting market landscape. One particular occurrence early on is that teams realize there's lots of money to be made in buying and reselling pigs, so they quickly begin to do so.

However, the railroad's need for pigs is quickly satisfied, at which point they will no longer purchase them. Unfortunately, the citizens of Rattlesnake Canyon are usually not adequately focused on the customer's needs (the railroad), being more concerned with what they feel is in their own best interest – buy and sell lots of pigs, fast!

The result is usually a glut of pigs available for sale, owned by merchants who can no longer sell them to the railroad, and by settlers who can no longer sell them to the merchants. There are too many pigs available, and no place to offload them! While this fact is slowly dawning on the "negotiators" on each team, the "buyers" on the teams are continuing to buy as many pigs as they can. Money is being wasted at a frantic rate until someone shouts out:

"We need to stop buying pigs!"

Once this message gets to all concerned, the pig-buying frenzy subsides and money continues to be spent on the dozens of other items still desperately needed by the customer. But the money spent on pigs is gone and the excess pigs remain just that – excess inventory with no further value. This is typically a painful realization for all who find themselves in that predicament.

This lesson about the need to be intimately aware of the needs of your customer, and immediately responsive to those needs, changing your own approach as the customer's needs change, is one of the principle debrief points from the experience.

The facilitator uses the example of the pigs to make the point and there is usually a collective groan from the room as most realize they ended the experience with far too many pigs. Now, when it's all over, they have a visceral appreciation of the importance of being truly customer focused...in practice, not just in theory!

After the training has long since been completed, there is still that common language and understanding in the organization. "We need to stop buying pigs!" spoken at a meeting, a conference, or between colleagues, immediately brings to mind the experience of Rattlesnake Canyon, and the lesson of being truly customer focused.

Those few words have meaningful personal significance to those who participated. Everyone knows what is meant: "**We must move off the seductive path of concentrating on what we feel is best and refocus on what the customer wants, responding to that need – and we need to respond quickly**."

This highlights the power of common language (everyone knows what "pigs" means), and common experience (everyone knows the folly of buying unwanted pigs).

Experiential learning provides this vehicle for introducing a common experience across a wide spectrum of the organization. It also gives participants a common language that is critical to optimizing results. These meanings would otherwise have to be conveyed by other, far less effective, and more time-consuming communication approaches.

◀ *Strongly themed images drive home the learning points of Rattlesnake Canyon through emails and personal screensavers.*

YOU ARE YOURSELF

I've touched on this earlier, but it is such an important aspect of experiential learning that a few additional thoughts may be of value.

Given how important it is for any learning to have a "practice" component, it is clearly most effective when that practice replicates true-to-life behavior. This is often difficult in a classroom, where the environment in which the practice occurs does not reflect the work environment.

When role-plays or other practice scenarios are used, then the situation in which the practice is occurring is nothing like the situation in which the participants will find themselves after the course. It is missing the impact of the work environment. As a result, the practice often appears sterile, or not very realistic or applicable.

The work environment is usually one with many competing priorities, intense time pressure, unexpected needs arising, and a scarcity of resources. Therefore, trying to learn, practice, and then apply new behaviors back on the job is not an easy task — the circumstances of the real world can make it very challenging! Yet, if the learning is only theory, then mastering those new behaviors in that pressure-filled environment is even less likely. Ideally, then, the practice would include an opportunity to develop the new skills in an environment that mimics the real world, before going back to the job.

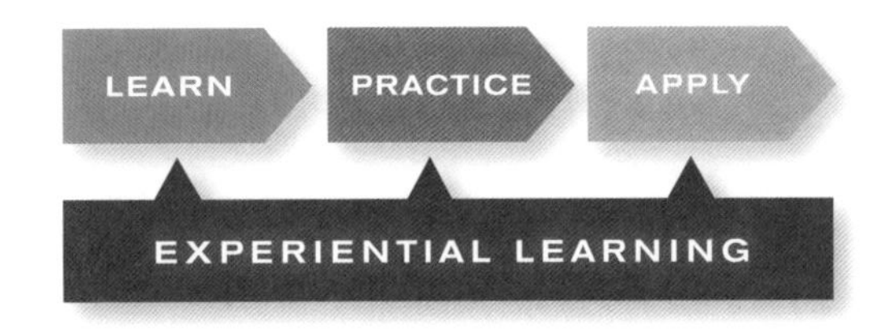

▲ *Experiential learning is impactful at all three stages of the competency improvement journey.*

This practice opportunity must also be one in which the participants are able to act as they normally would. Their approach to interpersonal relationships, team skills, communication skills, priority-setting capabilities, and leadership competencies all need to be given the opportunity to be used.

Participants need to practice new behaviors within the framework of their existing competencies if those new skills are to become part of their habitual repertoire.

▲ *The lessons of the experience have direct on-the-job application...how to "win" in the experience is the same way to "win" at work.*

Hence, two elements need to be in place when participants are attempting to move from hearing about what to do to actually doing it on the job. The first is that the practice environment needs to be similar to that in which the new skills will be applied. The second is that already existing capabilities need to have the same place during the practice as they'll have back on the job.

The value of experiential learning is that it addresses both of these requirements. The experience can create whatever environment is required...highly competitive, time sensitive, dependent on others, confusing, process oriented, or any one of several real-world situations. The experience can be structured to create the necessary environment that mirrors the participants' world, and so optimize the benefit of the practice.

In addition, the only constraints placed on participants within an experience are the operational guidelines or "rules," which apply equally to all involved. Beyond that, each person brings their own capabilities to the challenge of the experience. This allows for the new behaviors to be learned within the larger framework of each person's existing areas of competence.

Experiential learning allows each person to act as they would were they on the job, and then, within that paradigm, bring focus to what needs to be learned and mastered.

As a quick illustration, Eagle's Flight's Talon Technologies™ is an experience designed to allow participants the opportunity to practice continuous process- improvement principles.

In each of several phases, teams of six apply techniques that are taught just before that particular practice phase, and are given increasingly high expectations to be met. By the time the experience is over, participants not only have an understanding of what to do, they've actually done it repeatedly and seen dramatically improved results.

RED BLUE SILVER BLUE RED

However, as they work in teams and progressively apply the new learnings, they do it using all of their other existing competencies. The teamwork required draws on the same capabilities they would use back on the job. This applies similarly for their skills in the areas of planning, decision making, leadership, delegation, communication, meetings management, goal definition, etc. They bring themselves and their abilities to the experience. It's not seen as a game, a simulation, or a role-play. It is simply another experience.

The environment that is created replicates their real world, with similar pressures and accountabilities. It is immersive and all consuming, requiring that to succeed they not only apply the new behaviors being taught, but that they also tackle them the same way they'd tackle any work-related mandate. It's this mimicking of their reality, while still presenting the challenge in a fun and unique way, and yet with a totally different theme than they're used to, that gives experiential learning its great power and ability to help truly change behavior.

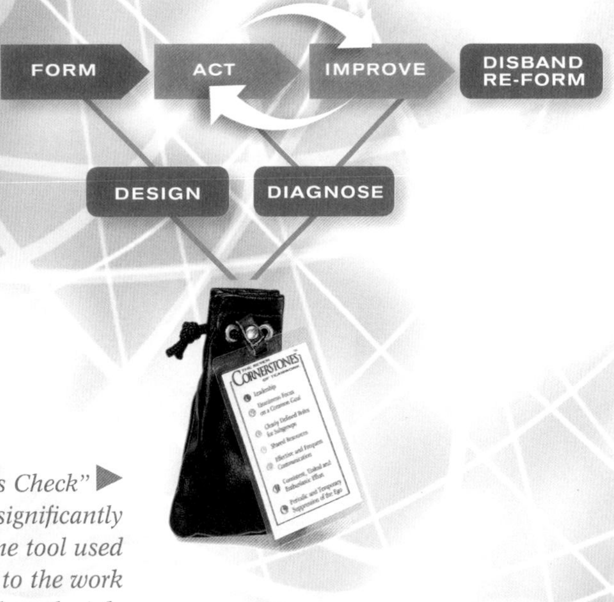

Making frequent use of a "Stones Check" diagnoses team effectiveness and significantly increases productivity. The same tool used to improve results is taken back to the work environment and used on the job.

THEMES

One of the niftiest things about both creating and participating in experiential learning events is their themes. They're always fun to work with as the designer, and they serve to capture the imagination of the participants.

They also play a very important role in making the experiential learning valuable, in that the theme creates the storyline and the metaphor that then unfolds during the experience, and in which the learning is embedded.

Disney has perfected this from an entertainment (vs. learning) perspective. There is a story behind each of their attractions, and this story serves to provide the detail and framework around which the attraction is developed. As a guest, regardless of the attraction you're about to experience, by the time you've made it to the head of the line the story has been brought to life.

They have posters on walls, old desks that you pass by which have been left just the way the "occupants" of that story would have left them, video which provides context for the attraction to come, and of course a building or environment in which the guest is immersed and that reflects the storyline.

Once you enter the attraction, the costumes, music, transportation, scripts, and special effects all bring the story to life. Each aspect of the attraction adds to the story in some way, so the guest is truly participating in that theme, not just going on a ride.

This same principle applies not only to their attractions, but to their hotels, restaurants, gardens, pools, and special events. There is a story or theme behind everything they do, which allows the guest to feel as though they are in far more than just a "location," but rather somewhere magical. They definitely understand the power of themes, and are masters at creating them.

An effective experience used to support corporate development also needs to be effectively themed. If it is, then the participants are able to accept the challenge, activity, or mandate posed by the experience as "real," and engage fully.

The theme does not have to be work related (e.g., running a factory), and in fact if it is slightly imaginary, it allows participants to enter into it as a real thing, but not so real as to make it simply a workplace simulation. It must be real enough to allow the participants to be themselves, and yet imaginary enough to become a comprehensive metaphor for the real world, and hence an effective learning vehicle.

It's in this balance that great experiences find their own magic as powerful, memorable, and engrossing tools. In the hands of a skilled facilitator, they significantly contribute to changed behavior.

▲ *Theme: Exciting European road rally*
Learning: Performance optimization

▲ *Theme: Environmental challenge to save the turtles*
Learning: Teamwork

◀ *Theme: Reconstruct an ancient archaeological discovery from cryptic notes*
Learning: Coaching

◀ *Theme: Professor Inno's Innovation Laboratory*
Learning: Mastering the innovation process

▶ *Theme: Make blockbuster movies by assembling the right cast for your film's genre.*
Learning: Resource optimization

Rattlesnake Canyon™ is set in the Old West where the sheriff – Sheriff Flynn – is also the town mayor and barber. He's good friends with Jackson Standish who owns a railroad back east and wants to expand. This friendship provides an opportunity for the good folks of Rattlesnake Canyon – both the settlers and the merchants – to benefit from the increased trade that a railroad through their town would offer; but they have to help the railroad company first by providing what it needs in the way of supplies.

From this theme is built out a full-blown experience that teaches about true partnerships in the world of sales, the importance of knowing and meeting customer needs, and the imperative of chasing maximum profit potential.

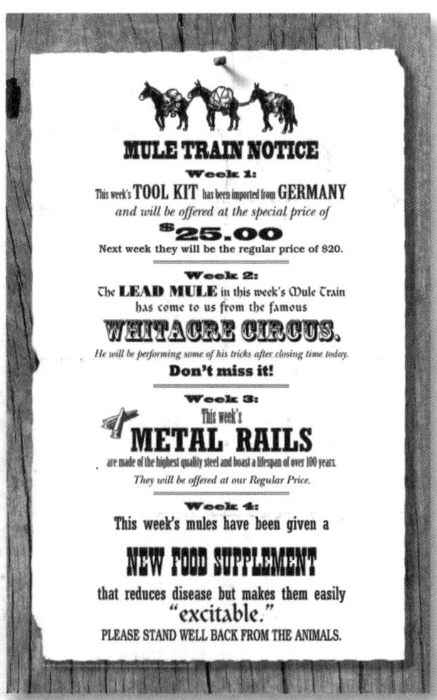

◀ *Through the use of images, the stage is set for the experience, creating a feeling of actually living and working in the town of Rattlesnake Canyon.*

▲ *Post-training material continues the metaphor to reinforce learnings.*

▲ *"Know Your Map" is one of the key learnings from Expedition Outback.*

Expedition Outback™
is set in the wilds of Australia, and allows participants many choices, and paths to optimum success, including kangaroos, diamonds, antidotes, and other related yet themed activities, like brushing kangaroo teeth! It provides a rich background for theming that is used to create great participant engagement.

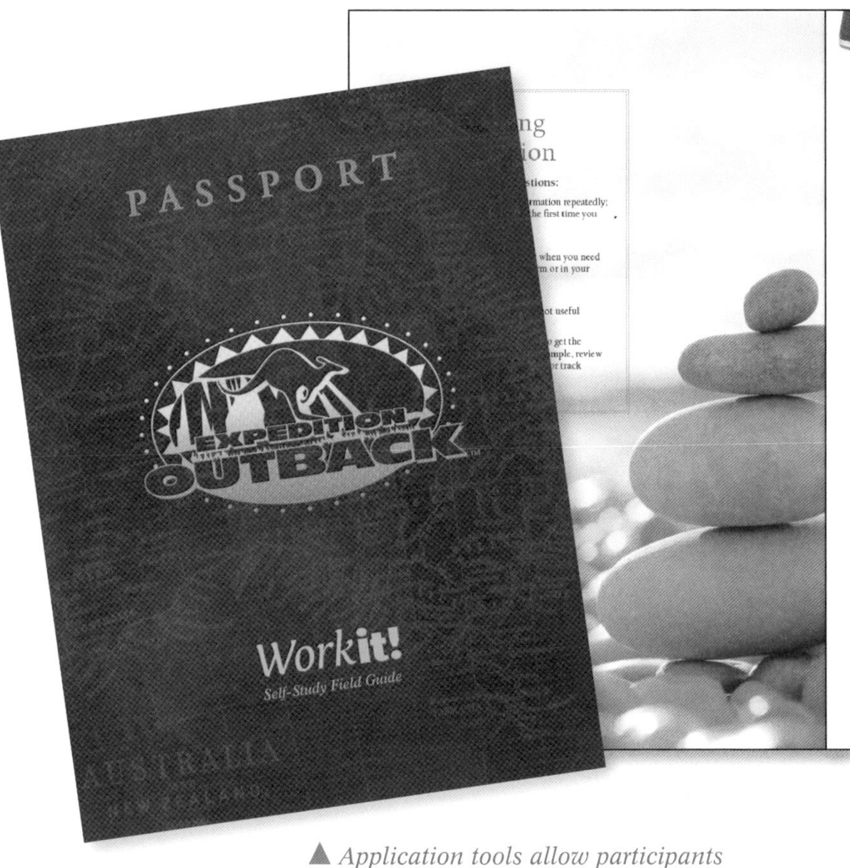

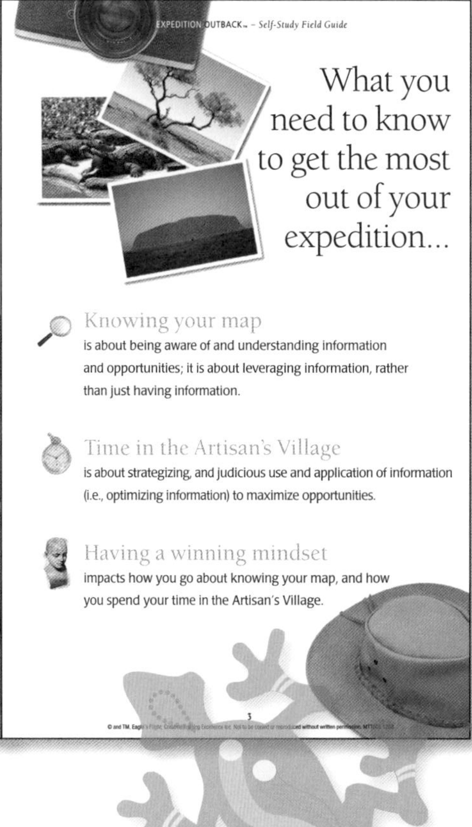

▲ *Application tools allow participants to directly apply the learnings on the job.*

Polar Frost™ is Expedition Outback™ brought from the wilds of Australia to the Canadian North – the same experience and learning, but simply re-themed.

Windjammer™, is set around the beautiful, warm, blue Caribbean ocean, and on the lush islands that draw the wealthy and talented oceangoing yachters and their sleek sailing crafts.

In one instance, a client was running a conference; they had already selected a theme, and it wasn't sailing. They asked if we could run exactly the same learnings and debrief, but theme the experience differently. We were able to do this by having our artists and developers write a new storyline – this time around mountain climbing – and then change each component of the experience (names of products, names of companies, language used, etc.) to match that new story. "Windjammer" became "Adrenaline Adventures."

Windjammer has undergone other transformations: to themes around rock climbing, mountain biking, and even a pet accessories company! The reverse has also been true. We've re-themed another experience set in the era of Camelot and made it into a sailing theme!

The principle is that the learnings of each experience don't change, but the clothes, or theme, in which those learnings are addressed, can be effectively altered to whatever optimizes the experience and the learning impact for the participants.

5 THEMES
for the same experience, created in response to client needs

"BUT I DON'T
LIKE GAMES!"

REDLINE
RACING

Periodically, but not as often as one would think, we hear "But I don't like games" from a participant, or relayed through HR to us from potential participants.

A similar comment that we very often hear before a session where experiential learning is being used for the first time is:

"THIS HAD BETTER WORK...MY CAREER IS ON THE LINE HERE!"

In both cases, once the session is over, the feedback comments are always something like:

"THAT WAS GREAT! PROBABLY THE **BEST** TRAINING WE'VE EVER HAD."

REDLINE RACING.
Australian Tour
REDLINE
RACING.

REDLINE RACING.
Asian Tour
REDLINE
RACING.

REDLINE RACING.
South African Tour
REDLINE
RACING.

It's true that experiential learning does use games, but they are more like experiences in which people are quickly caught up with delivering the required outcome. They are immediately absorbed by the challenge, adventure, mission, or mandate, and respond accordingly. The theme which gives the experience its gamelike feel remains, but is now linked to the expected outcome they have to deliver.

It's only when the debrief begins that they fully appreciate the value of the theme, and the metaphor for reality that the gamelike appearance has provided.

A "game" typically has little semblance of reality, cannot be debriefed to any depth, and has as its objective an entertaining way to pass the time. An experience, on the other hand, while it may be called a game by the participants, is really a wolf in sheep's clothing. It looks superficially like a game, but is quickly recognized to be, in fact, a meaningful challenge, requiring application of all one's skills. Its purpose is to intimately support changed behavior that will improve corporate performance.

So...to the comment "I don't like games," we usually say something like "Duly noted. Please bear with us for a few minutes and then we'll see if you feel that this is really the kind of game you don't like."

Shortly thereafter, the rules and the challenge have been understood, and everyone is fully engaged. I do think initial responses like "I don't like games," or "This had better work" are fair, and should be respected. They shouldn't be a reason for not using experiential learning in training events, but that viewpoint should be understood. There are many who have simply never participated in a true experiential learning activity. Others may think they have, but it really wasn't one. It may have been called that, but in reality was simply an (indoor or outdoor) activity followed by a debrief with limited effectiveness or relevance.

On the other hand, those who have experienced the power of this kind of learning become advocates for it, and typically feel that the "game in the course" was the best part of the training and brought the most value to the day.

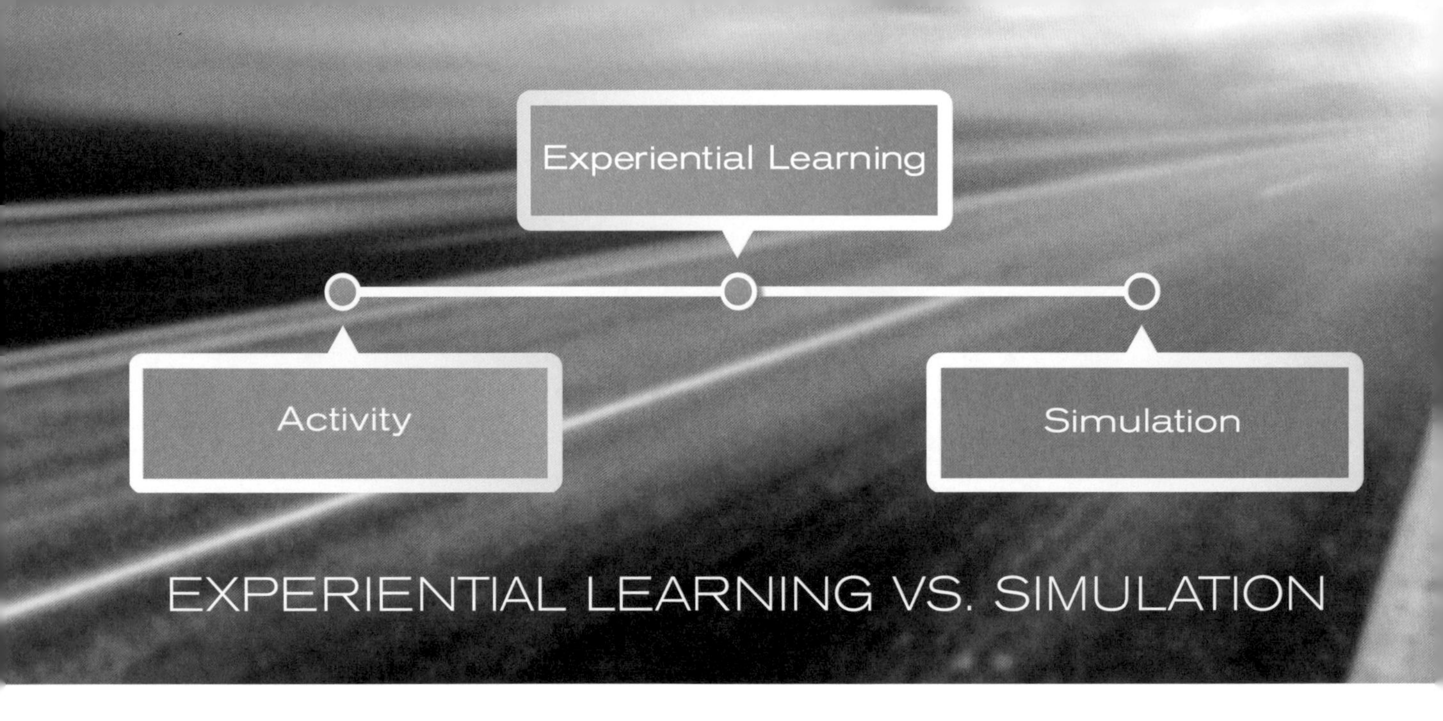

EXPERIENTIAL LEARNING VS. SIMULATION

There are many who use the terms "Experience" and "Simulation" interchangeably as a way to describe what I would call experiential learning. However, there is a difference, and for the sake of clarity I would use the terms differently.

Consider a spectrum. A training "Activity" would be at the far left-hand end, a "Simulation" at the far right-hand end, and "Experiential Learning" would sit in the middle.

ACTIVITY

Training activities are usually short exercises used to illustrate some point. They are generally generic, in that participants are simply asked something like: "What did you learn?" and most of their answers will be okay.

An example would be the "trust fall" where participants allow themselves to fall backward into the hands of other participants. The observations all revolve around some form of discussion about trust.

Another example would be where participants are put into teams and given a puzzle to solve together, and are then asked about their observations around teamwork.

SIMULATION

A simulation is an exact replica of the participants' work environment and usually used to teach mastery of complex skills. It's typically quite long, very involved, and uniquely job specific. The goal is for participants to literally acquire mastery of some difficult and complex tasks or skills.

An example would be the simulators used in the airline industry to train pilots. They allow for mastery of any situation that a pilot might encounter on a routine flight, and then virtually all other situations that they could conceivably encounter. Once they've mastered these skills in the simulator, they can move to the cockpit of an actual plane; but, once there, it will look and feel identical to the simulator.

Another example would be in the fast-food industry. An actual restaurant is built at the training facility, and managers and employees are trained there on how to run a restaurant, but in a simulated environment. They learn to do exactly the same thing in the simulation that they will do once in an actual restaurant.

EXPERIENTIAL LEARNING

Experiential learning sits in the middle of this spectrum, as it both provides a nonrelated work activity from which to learn, and also simulates reality in that what is learned has direct and predictable application back on the job.

An experience usually runs for one to two hours followed by an extensive debrief. The facilitator draws out the predetermined learnings from the participants themselves and then elaborates on them. From there, application to on-the-job reality is made.

As an illustration of experiential learning, Eagle's Flight has an experience in which participants must act as an elite team providing on-site research stations in the challenging environment that exists in a tropical jungle. They work for a worldwide conglomerate called **Alpha Wave**™, and this particular project has been named **Jungle 3**™.

In it, they are tasked with deciding which research stations to build and where, bearing in mind the company's established minimum requirements. In addition, they must adhere to stringent safety standards, bearing in mind the likelihood of serious threats posed by such a hostile environment, as well as Alpha Wave's need to optimize profit on the project.

There are several resources available to them to facilitate success, and teams are able to assess the relative value of each against the time constraints of the project, and then select and use them accordingly. Decisions taken wisely lead to ongoing positive returns for the company. Unwise decisions attract consequences which must be dealt with, often resulting in lost time and money. All these opportunities, issues, and challenges exist concurrently during the course of the hour-long experience.

The real-world application focuses on accountability. Teams experience the same pressures in the experience that they do on the job. They must deliver on key metrics, optimize results, select and utilize the appropriate support available, (while contending with the consequences of their actions and decisions), and yet still be held accountable to the required end results.

Accountability is a key challenge in today's work environment, as individuals come to recognize that "trying" is not the same as "guaranteeing" when it comes to promised outcomes. Alpha Wave not only brings this message to the forefront, but goes on to teach some key behaviors which, when adopted, can greatly facilitate delivery of accountabilities. These include principles such as "First know, then follow, not first do, then fix," "Accountability is a choice," and "First consider consequence." Alpha Wave simulates reality, but does so in what is perceived to be a game, but from which participants learn. It is truly "experiential learning."

In Summary

Each of these three forms of training (Activity, Simulation, and Experiential Learning) has its own value and place. Generally, though, experiential learning is the most versatile and engaging of the three. The exception to this is when an actual simulation is specifically called for, such as the example of training pilots in an accurately simulated cockpit environment.

ALPHAWAVE
JUNGLE
First Know,
Then Follow
NOT
First Do,
Then Fix
Never Let a Teammate Fail
1
2
3
4

THE DEBRIEF

ndjammer
g the Wind of Opportunity
The Five Navigation Buoys of Success
For each of the following Five Navigation Buoys, rate your performance as a crew during Windjammer using the following rating scale:
1 On the Reef
2 Hard to Port
3 Clear Sailing
4 Dolphins off the Port Bow
5 Wind in Your Sails
The Five Navigation Buoys of Success
Hit every high point.
Plan all ten rounds.
Use the crew wisely.
Build with all five colors.
Change the sails with changing
Performance Analysis
Generally speaking, on which products did you concentrate, and when?
Product 1 The Wanderer
Product 2 The Wood Duck
Product 3 The White Squall
Product 4 The Windham
Product 5 The Westford
Early on
In the middle
At the end
Opportunity Analysis
Value Analysis, circle the places on the Market Value
missed opportunities to make a significant profit.
Product 5 The Westford

When an archer uses a bow, the single objective is to send the arrow to the target. However, after notching, the arrow's success is dependent on two things: first, fully drawing back the bowstring, and then second, releasing it well.

The use of experiential learning also has a single goal: to support the objective of changed behavior to the benefit of the organization. However, as with the bow, success with experiential learning is also dependent on two things: the experience itself, and then the debrief that follows.

With the archer, it does no good to only pull back the bowstring, no matter how well it's done, or how true the aim. Nor can the archer be successful if, once pulled, the bowstring and arrow are not then skillfully released towards the target.

With the facilitator, there must first be a powerful and relevant experience. Once the experience is done, though, it is of no real use without a clear and relevant debrief. The two go hand in hand. A great experience without a correspondingly great debrief is really little more than a game; but a great delivery of content without an experience is essentially nothing more than yet another PowerPoint presentation.

▲ *This arrow and plaque are handed out to participants as the key learning tool from "The Leaders Imperatives," a program which focuses on accountability.*

So, the debrief is an equally vital component to the success of an experiential learning event. The formula we use at Eagle's Flight to ensure that this occurs is: "How to win in the game...how to win at work." The way this formula is implemented is illustrated by the following diagrams.

The first step is to recognize that there are three distinct components to any experiential learning activity.

1. **The actual experience itself.** This can be either short or long, embedded in the larger course or used as a stand-alone event, and done for a large group or a small one.

2. **Next is the debrief.** Again, depending on need, time constraints, the purpose of the experiential learning event, and the other course components, the debrief can be relatively short, extended, or very extensive. It can be done in a single block of time, over time, or woven throughout the learning that will follow; and it can be done by a facilitator, or team taught with others.

3. **The third component is the application.** Here the facilitator links the material presented when debriefing the experience to the participants' real world, and outlines how to apply the debrief points to their on-the-job reality. This includes what to do differently, and how, in order to make a significant and positive impact on the organization.

These three components are then brought to life for the participants as follows.

1. HOW TO WIN IN THE GAME

Bear in mind that the participants have just been totally immersed in a compelling and all-consuming activity. They've had to learn the rules, tackle the challenge, interact with others, and then receive the fruits of their labors. They've shifted their thinking from their work environment to the experience's theme. They have definitely been both emotionally and physically involved, and personally invested in achieving the best possible outcome.

When the experience is over, they will want (after a few minutes taken for a well-deserved break) to know exactly what just happened. At this point they really haven't had a chance to pause and see the larger picture. Also, they will want to know "how they did," and then immediately after that...how they could have done better!

So, after they come back from the break, the first action of the facilitator is to allow them to "catch their breath," what we at Eagle's Flight call "a chance to decompress." We usually do this by beginning with a question like: "What do you think this experience was all about?" We then allow a few minutes for them to talk together in their teams, at their tables.

There may be one or two similar general questions given to them until the facilitator feels that the group has "come back to reality," and has stepped back somewhat from their intense involvement with the experience.

After capturing their thinking from those first couple of questions, the facilitator then moves to a comprehensive debrief where they uncover what behaviors they would have needed to exhibit to really "win in the game." In those cases where the goal is for skills to be built, the debrief is around "what skills did they need to learn to win?"

They've played the game, and now it's human nature to want to know how to win. At this point they don't realize that "winning" in the game uses the same principles that they will need to "win" at work. Consequently, at this step the facilitator must make each of these components very clear.

This is a very important first step, because it's here that each component expressly designed into the experience to change behavior is discussed, and shown to be a critical element for success in the game. Later they'll come to understand that it is also a critical capability to have back on the job.

As an example, in the Eagle's Flight experience **Promises, Promises!**™ success comes from the discipline not to "throw scandals" at other "countries." In the game, the use of scandals, while very clearly optional, is always an action that participants take early in the experience. As a result, a number of unwanted but inevitable consequences occur, and the required outcome appears to be impossible to achieve.

In the debrief (which, in this experience, actually begins mid game, although the participants don't realize it), the facilitator points out this truth: Throwing scandals is extremely counterproductive, and in fact makes achievement of the mandate impossible.

From that, the participants return to the game with an altered viewpoint and ultimately conclude, as a group, to forgo further use of "scandals" (which are represented in Promises, Promises! by colorful koosh balls), and are then able to achieve a successful outcome. This is an excellent example of the facilitator initially showing participants how to win in the game – get rid of all koosh balls (scandals) before doing anything else at all. This will build trust, and lay the foundation for ultimate success for everyone.

▶ This is a reinforcement tool reminding participants to apply the learning from the experience of "Promises, Promises!."

◀ "Scandals" are being managed by an Ambassador to the United League of Nations.

2. HOW TO WIN AT WORK

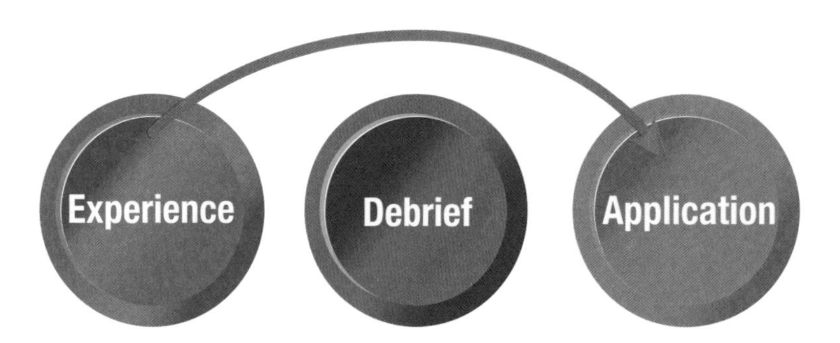

Once each of the principles that are key to success in the game has been explained, and brought to life at the personal level for the participants, the facilitator then shifts them back to their real world – the world of work for which the experience was merely a metaphor.

Each principle of success is then revisited and linked back to their on-the-job reality.

Two points are key here. The first is that considerable work needs to be done in advance to customize this aspect of the debrief. Examples used must be accurate, and ones with which participants identify. The language used must be the same used in the organization. Company values, strategies, competitors, customers, and priorities must all be referenced and incorporated. **The debrief must link exactly and directly to what they deal with every day.**

The second is that in both the "how to win in the game" portion of the debrief, and then again in the "how to win at work" section, the facilitator isn't simply expounding. For the participants to get maximum benefit, the debrief must also include considerable opportunity for individuals to participate and talk together. There are several ways to do this, but what they all have in common is that the participants have time to personally process the information, work in teams at their tables, and share their observations in dialogue both with other groups and with the facilitator, who can then comment in response.

The job of the facilitator is to bring the metaphor of the experience to life for each participant, showing what to do differently and, critically, the impact of doing it differently back at work. The same desire each person brings to succeed in the game, they bring to their job; however, they now know more clearly how to guarantee that success.

Many of our facilitators will ask at this point: **"Have you ever played this game before?"** and the answer is usually "No." The facilitator then challenges that answer saying: "You may not have realized it, but you play this game every day. The theme is different, but the rules are the same, and the goal is the same. Now, going forward, if you play it differently using what we've just discussed, you will play it much better."

▼ *After the experience, participants complete an application mat where they translate the learnings from the experience to their on-the-job performance.*

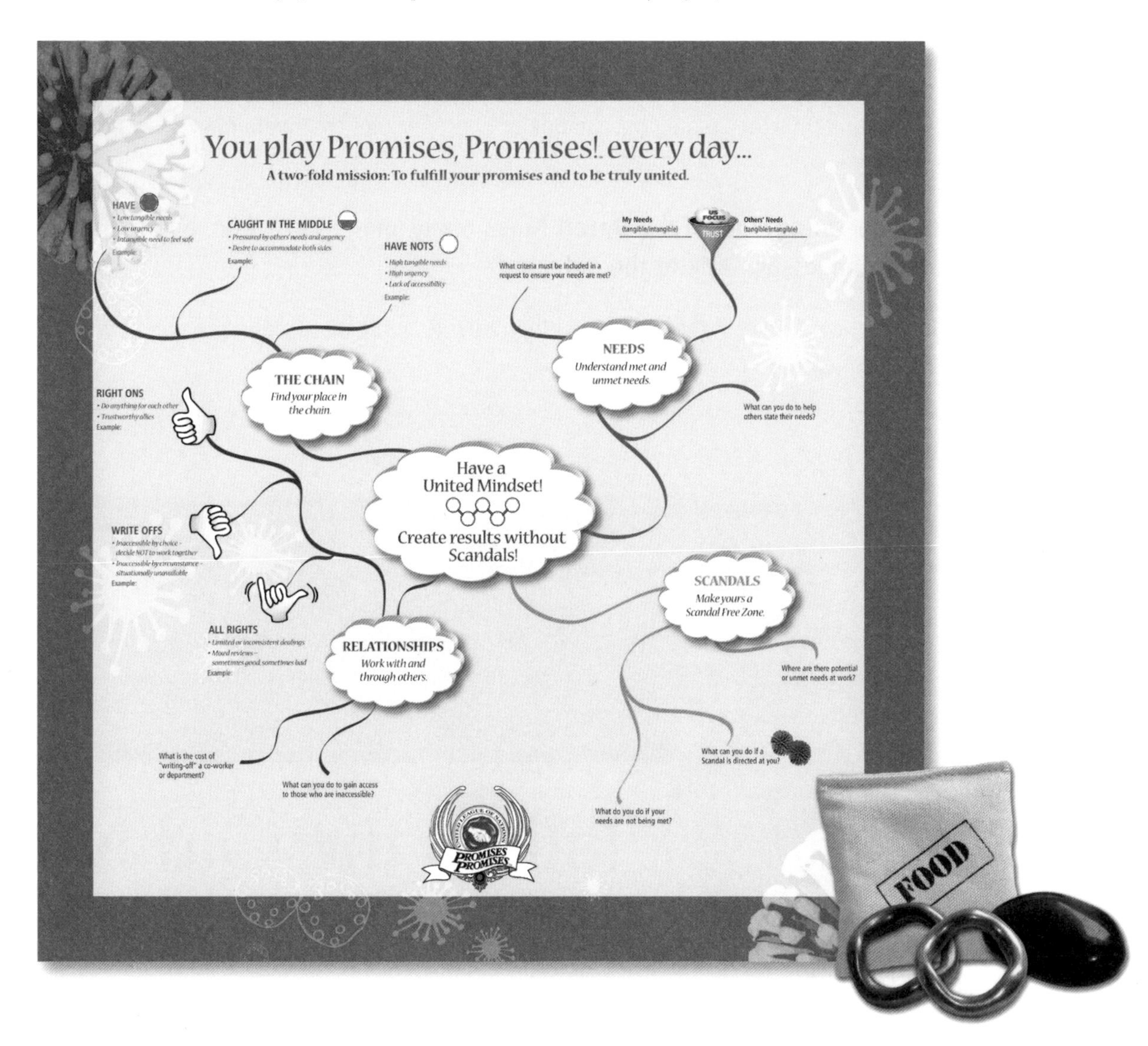

From there, participants are asked to reflect on what they'll now do differently, starting immediately, and then discuss those commitments at their tables.

Experience
Debrief
Application

Clearly the success of the experiential learning event is tied heavily to the debrief. It must be relevant, build off of the experience they just had, and make very explicit what are the things to do differently tomorrow.

An interesting aside here: whenever we run into someone who has participated in this level of experiential learning event, even years later, they often remember it. They remember the experience, and more importantly they remember the one or two principles that were most relevant to them at the time.

"I remember doing Gold of the Desert Kings many, many years ago, and I still remember the lesson...talk to the old man!"

Showing first how to win in the game, and then how to apply that learning to win at work, is extremely powerful!

What current project would benefit from your asking, "What's possible"?

Talk to the Old Man.

Configurations™

An illustration of the experiential learning process

Eagle's Flight has a relatively short experience called **Configurations**™, around the topic of Communication Effectiveness. It takes about 10 minutes to give participants the guidelines they must follow, then the experience usually lasts about 45 minutes. Within that time there are three rounds, with time between each round for the teams to self-diagnose, and plan how to proceed to the next round. The debrief usually then takes about another 45 minutes.

The participants work in teams of three or four, and the goal is to complete that particular round as quickly as possible. Typically we encourage some friendly competition between the teams to add a heightened sense of urgency, and to reflect that they face competition every day within their organizations.

Three Rounds

On average, teams will take about 10 minutes to complete round 1. Once they have finished, they are provided with the opportunity to talk amongst themselves in answer to the facilitator's question: "What can you do differently to cut your time score in half in the next round?" Once they're ready they move to round 2. The guidelines they must follow remain the same as in round 1, but the task itself is somewhat more complicated.

After round 2, they compare their time scores to what they achieved in round 1 and usually have cut their time in half or better...a significant improvement. They are once again given the opportunity to discuss amongst themselves how to improve their performance even more in the third round.

At the end of this last planning discussion, the facilitator then hears from each group what they did differently between rounds 1 and 2, and what they now plan to do differently in round 3. This provides an opportunity for everyone to learn from one another, and share what is emerging as best practices.

PARTICIPANTS CHANGED THEIR BEHAVIOR BETWEEN EACH ROUND, AND AS A RESULT PERFORMANCE IMPROVED...RADICALLY!

Before starting round 3, they are given some additional time to consider what they just heard, and decide if they'd like to incorporate anything further into their own approach.

Round 3 begins, again with a slightly harder task than in round 2. This time teams typically finish within 2 or 3 minutes, with some outstanding teams getting their times down to the one-minute mark!

They changed their behavior between each round, and as a result their performance improved...radically!

Experiential Learning in Action

Before discussing the debrief, it's worth noting that during the course of the experience participants discovered for themselves, with limited facilitator involvement, how they thought they could improve. They also had to decide if they felt that implementing those observations would in fact improve their results and, if so, how they'd go about it. They then made the changes to their own behaviors and saw improved performance.

Because of this process – where the learning was personal and visceral – conviction developed about what could be achieved if different behaviors were adopted, knowledge of how to make the changes surfaced, skills to do so were crafted, and then the results were seen. This is Heart, Head, Hands, Harvest in action, and shows the actual power of experiential learning.

Furthermore, the facilitator knew exactly what would be learned by the participants, when they would discover these truths, and how they would then apply them. This was not something that "just happened." Rather, the experience was designed to achieve a particular outcome, and it did so far more effectively than by simply "telling" the participants the information they discovered on their own; in fact, telling them how they should change their behavior would probably have had little or no impact at all.

The Debrief

In the debrief, the facilitator probes more deeply about their observations between rounds, allowing them to understand more fully what happened, using questions like the following:

"What did you do differently between each round? Why?"

"What old ways of behaving did you replace with what new ways to see such a significant improvement in results?"

"Why were you willing to change your behavior as the experience progressed?"

"What was difficult to address as you moved from round to round? What was easy? Why?"

The objective of these kinds of questions is, as much as possible, to allow participants to discover the key learning principles for themselves, and be able to link them back to the experience.

The facilitator then codifies these learnings by articulating the principles behind the improved performance. In this experience there are ten principles, but depending on time and desired focus, usually three dominate.

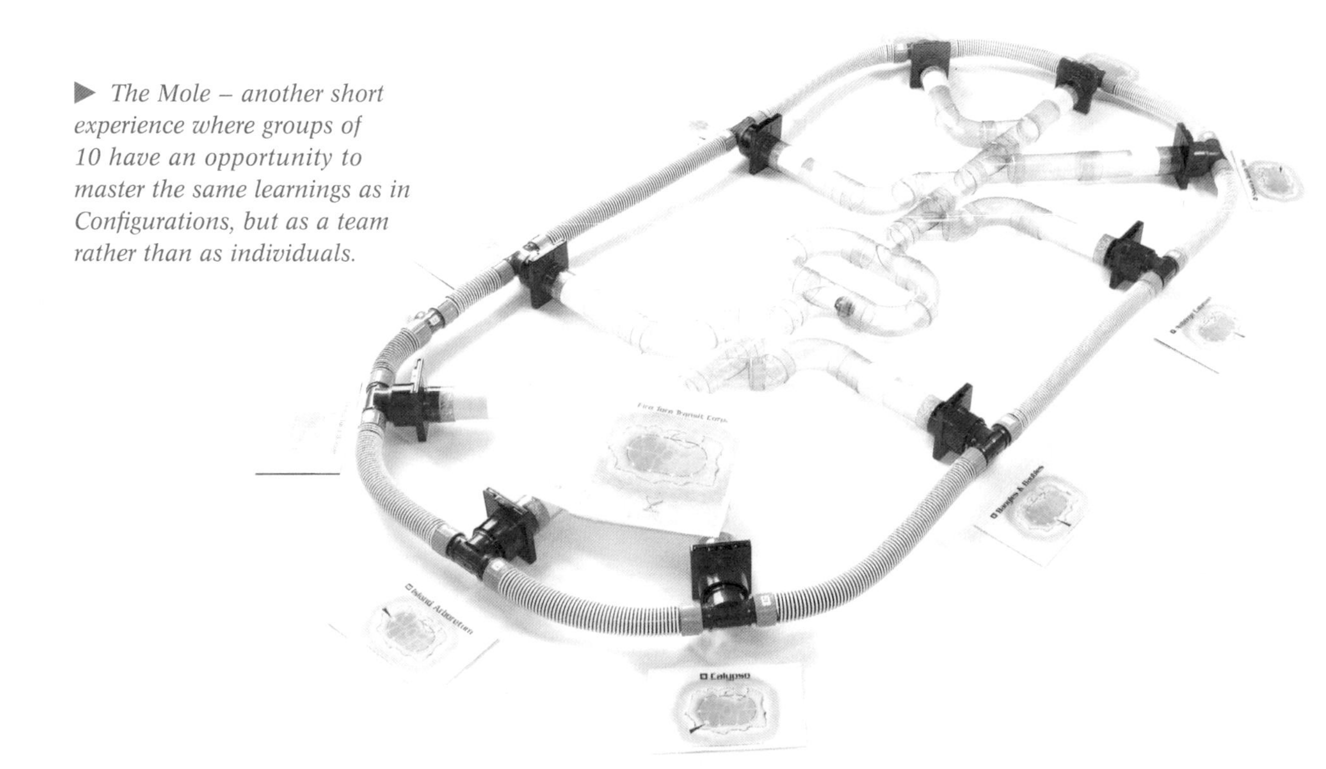

▶ *The Mole – another short experience where groups of 10 have an opportunity to master the same learnings as in Configurations, but as a team rather than as individuals.*

Results

As the experience progressed from round to round, the focus on improved results allowed the team to shift from personal approaches and agendas to the common focus of improving results. So at work, when the sole focus becomes to produce brilliant results, all other considerations fall by the wayside. The objective then is to know what brilliant looks like and put all collective energy towards achieving that.

"Tap In"

This is a term introduced during the experience that means any other team member has the freedom to interject with feedback at the very moments when they feel that feedback will help. As the rounds progressed, this Tapping In became increasingly frequent, and so results continued to improve.

Initially there was resistance to Tapping In, either out of respect for what someone else on the team was doing (even if it was becoming counterproductive, but being done with good intentions), or because of a lack of personal conviction about the degree of value it would add. As the experience progressed, the value of giving individual feedback was increasingly realized, and doing so was not seen as offensive or unwanted.

The reason for this is that Tapping In was being recognized as a powerful way to improve results, and as that became more important and a greater focus, the tools for achieving it were seen as increasingly valuable.

The Best Leaders Give and Get Constant Feedback

The Best Leaders Use Common Language

▲ *An application of Configurations to Leadership.*

▶ *Three key learnings from Configurations.*

TAP IN
Constant Feedback

This is similarly true at work. When you see that a team member (or someone for whom you have responsibility as a coach) could improve performance, Tapping In is a powerful tool; as long as results are truly the focus for all concerned, it is always appreciated.

"Common Language"

Configurations is fundamentally about learning how to leverage the power of effective interactive communication opportunities. Within the experience, all team members come with their own way of expressing ideas, describing the actual component pieces of the experience, and making their personal points of view known.

Participants quickly realize that there is very little in the way of a truly common understanding of what is meant when others express themselves. Each is doing their best to be clear, and because all are using the English language, they assume that others understand, or at least that they are making themselves understood. It seems a bit far-fetched to say we don't share a common language.

However, after round 1 it is very clear that what we share are common words, but not a common understanding of what each of us means by the words we're using, or the intention behind how we put them together into sentences.

Much of the discussion that occurs among the team members between rounds 1 and 2 centers around getting a common meaning around the common words. Once this is clear then performance improves dramatically.

It's a very surprising revelation for participants that what they thought was very clear to others (because it was clear to themselves) was not in fact that clear. Bringing this understanding back to the job can be transformative, as people realize that much more effort needs to go into truly ensuring a common language, and that doing so has such a positive impact on improved performance.

On-The-Job-Application

After examining these principles in depth, showing how they were key to performance improvement in the experience and how they could be applied back on the job, the facilitator moves to personal application with questions similar to the following:

"Based on what you've learned from Configurations, what will you do differently once you're back at work, beginning immediately?"

"What hurdles do you foresee? How will you overcome these?"

"What impact will you have on improving results once these principles are part of your regular behavior?"

Participants commit to a course of action, share it with their teammates, and then own personal implementation of the promised outcome.

I once ran this experience for a group of senior European executives. I was only with them for a short time, as long as it took for the experience and debrief, in fact. They had never really had any form of experiential learning in the past; so, while not exactly skeptical, they were certainly curious. It seemed to go very well, and I felt that they had gained a lot of value; but as soon as I was done my part I left, and their meeting continued for the rest of the day.

Later, two interesting outcomes materialized. I met with one of the most senior of the group who, on reflecting on that meeting and the experience I had taken them through, commented that it was perhaps the most powerful and impactful training experience he had ever had. The second was that the group then authorized a much more comprehensive and widespread training initiative, explicitly using experiential learning, because of the impact that small taste had had on them.

I was pleased to get the feedback (and the business!), but was also reminded again of the power of experiential learning.

▶ *These are the key learning from a full-day leadership program in which Configurations is a component.*

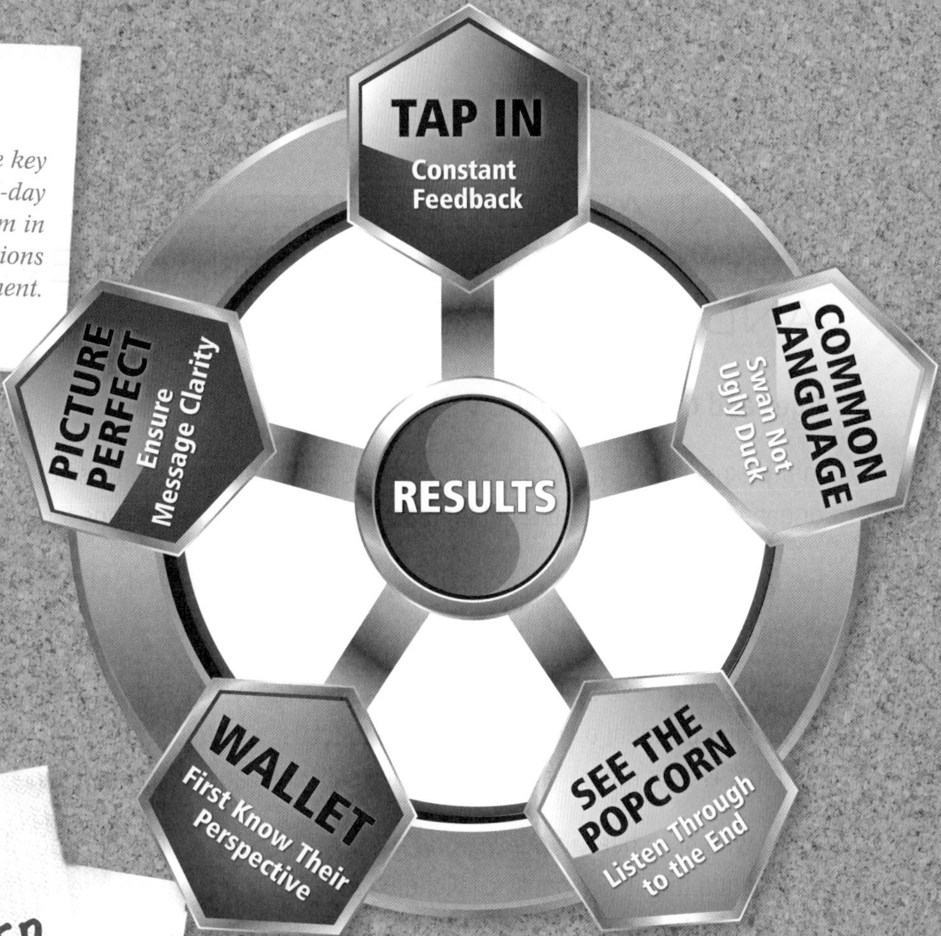

NAPKIN BASED COACHING

◀ *One way to apply Configurations back on the job on a daily basis.*

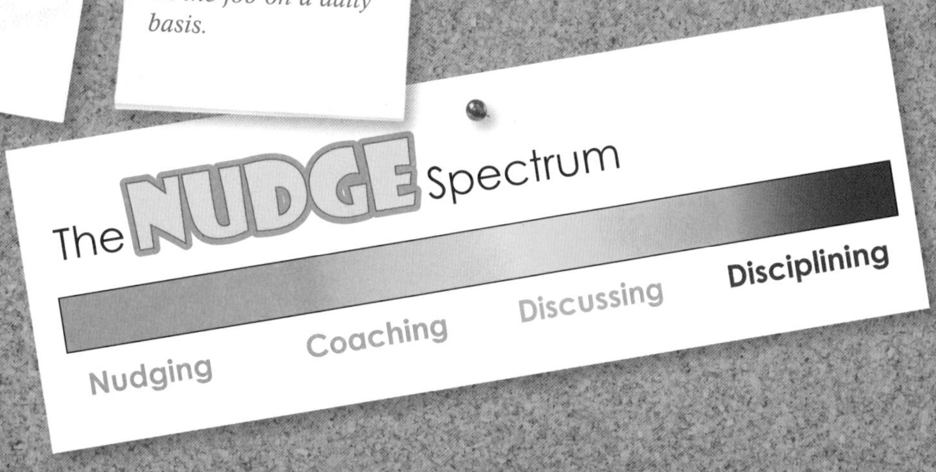

WHAT ABOUT DIFFERENT AGES, ORGANIZATIONAL LEVELS, AND CULTURES?

Ages and Organizational Levels

In my experience, experiential learning is equally effective regardless of the age or generational classification of the participants. I think the reasons for this are many.

For those newly entering the workforce, the idea of games and self-learning through personal experience is the norm for this generation.

For those who have been in the workforce for a few years, the opportunity for self-discovery and taking personal ownership of where to focus, which is at the heart of experiential learning, is their natural approach to the challenges and assignments they tackle.

Those who have been in the workforce for several years readily embrace the opportunity for learning that is personally challenging and involving, having already had an excess of "PowerPoint training."

▶ *Eagle's Flight is represented around the world where experiential learning is always equally well received.*

▲ *A 350 ft. bridge built by 700 participants in Dubai, UAE.*

As for senior executives, this group already has a number of well-honed skills and they prefer to learn through discussion with peers, sharing observations or viewpoints on principles presented. The challenge afforded by experiential learning immediately allows them a framework for this kind of training.

I think that a common reason for the universal acceptance of using experiences as a part of the training plan is that we as individuals, regardless of age or rank, always learn best by doing, always prefer doing over listening, and would always select being personally engaged and stimulated over being lectured to or taught. When the "teaching" then follows as part of something they've just completed – the debrief that follows – then it's seen to be practical and immediately relevant.

In addition, regardless of age or position, performance improvement and optimizing impact is an ongoing priority. Executives are looking to increase shareholder value, senior managers are striving to improve corporate performance metrics, mid-level employees are charged with improving efficiency and effectiveness measures, and those early in their career are focused on delivering and improving on defined targets.

The whole point of any form of development is to help the workforce meet, and if possible exceed, objectives. When training successfully does that, then it's adding real value. Because experiential learning is so effective at supporting this requirement, independent of where a person is operating within the company, it is readily accepted and embraced by all levels – and it is fun, which everyone always appreciates.

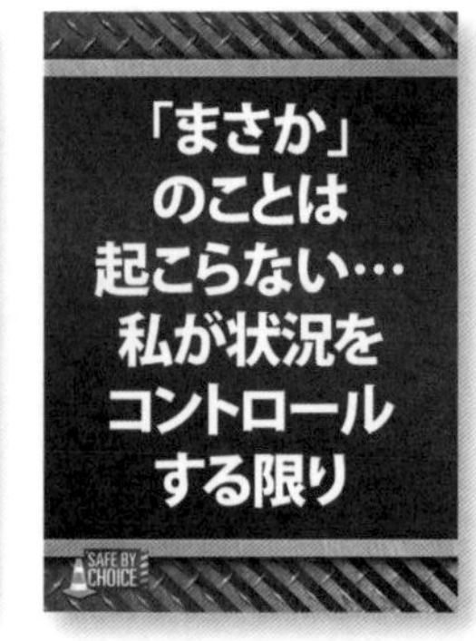

▲ *The key principles from any experience are usually simply expressed, and therefore easily translated.*

Different Cultures

Eagle's Flight currently operates in over 35 countries, and does so with equal success in each one. As an experiential learning company that relies heavily on experiences and related debriefs, that success is testament to the universality of this form of learning, and its ability to work well regardless of culture.

There are two observations that explain this reality.

1. The first is that all participants around the world are just people, regardless of nationality, and all prefer learning where they can be more involved in the process, being themselves, and learning by doing rather than listening.

2. The second is that experiential learning has at its core the fact that it uses principles to change behavior. These are internalized and then applied to an individual's work situation as they best see fit. This is in contrast to providing a list of dos and don'ts that must be remembered and followed, and which clearly can't cover every eventuality or circumstance.

The principles are embedded in the experience, drawn out in the debrief, and then made relevant to the workplace. Applying them improves performance, and since the discovery of these principles was a result of participating in the experience, they resonate, and are recognized as being worth personally adopting.

Principles understood, accepted, and then implemented are crucial to achieving consistently demonstrated changed behavior, which in turn further supports the priorities of the organization.

One important requirement, though, is that the debrief, and at times the rules, be partially customized or adapted to reflect the culture of the country in which they're being delivered. This is managed by the facilitator, and is easily done when the facilitator is local to the country, or has been briefed by someone local.

1. An example would be that in some countries "losing" a game can cause loss of face; in this case the teams can simply play on their own, and not be placed in competition with one another.
2. Another example would be the dominant force of existing hierarchies, when a more senior person's opinion will always be given preference. In this case, teams would be made up comprised only of peers, and not allowed to form randomly, thereby removing the risk of having senior people on teams simply giving direction.
3. A third example would be that in some countries people are exceptionally outgoing and social. In these cases their need to discuss and interact amongst themselves is high, so the facilitator will allow for that, either by giving more time for team discussion, or more opportunities.

Are we doing the right thing?
Gehen wir richtig vor?
¿Estamos haciendo lo correcto?
Faisons-nous ce qu'il faut ?
Doen we het juiste?
Facem ceea ce trebuie?

4. As a last example, in some countries people tend to be less social, and more about things needing to be "cut and dried," or more "black and white." In this case the facilitator would allow less discussion time, and focus more heavily on the scores and results obtained in the experience, and the implications behind those results.

In each of these cases the experience itself doesn't change, nor do the principles it teaches. What does change is the approach the local facilitator takes to draw out the learnings, in order to be respectful of the values, culture, and language (meanings of words) indigenous to each country or region.

A Cultural Bridge

One interesting and positive aside related to culture is that experiential learning is also a powerful way to bridge different cultures. Multinational organizations that bring people together from around the world can use it very effectively to create a common metaphor and understanding among many, in a manner that is not really possible to do as effectively in any other way.

As an example, one of our senior facilitators was required to run a very challenging and intense experience for several people from a single company, but who themselves came from many different countries within the Middle East. The required learning was the importance of collaboration and the imperative of not only meeting local objectives, but also being equally focused on achieving the larger corporate commitments through cross-country communication and cooperation.

Given that the citizens of these counties were, in some cases, literally at war with one another, and in others shared a great deal of bad feeling, the facilitator felt that she had her work seriously cut out for her in the best-case scenario, and faced certain failure in the worst!

The participants graciously gave full attention to the rules, and were committed to at least participate in the experience. At the end of the experience, they came to the personal realization that despite what was going on in their countries, they should, and could, work together for the common good of all.

This was a great example of experiential learning being able to transcend individual cultures when used in the hands of a highly skilled facilitator.

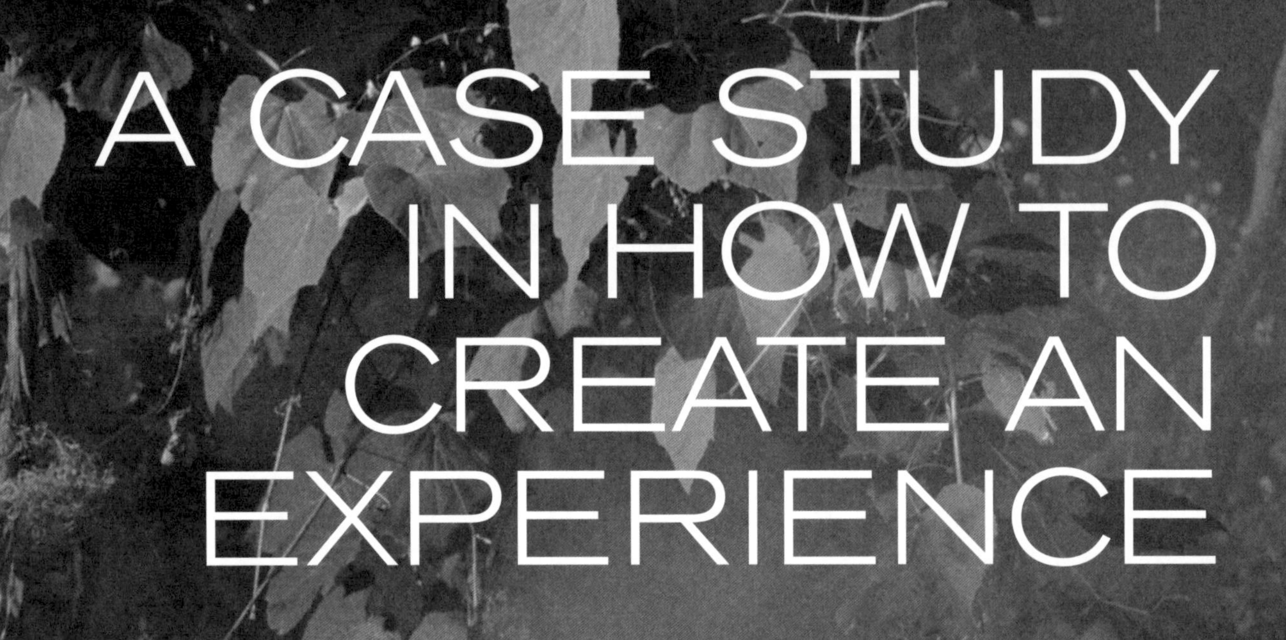

A CASE STUDY IN HOW TO CREATE AN EXPERIENCE

In this section I've laid out the steps I follow to create an experiential learning program. Eagle's Flight offers a workshop on how to do this, and this section covers the highlights from that course.

1. **What's the objective?**
2. **What components of the learning will be in the experience?**
3. **What kinds of environments naturally lend themselves to these behaviors?**
4. **What kind of theme will best serve the experience?**
5. **Give it a title.**
6. **Create a rough outline that brings it together.**
7. **Add specific detail of what needs to be taught.**
8. **Work out the numbers.**
9. **Test, rework, test, rework...**
10. **Prepare the rules to be delivered in an entertaining and effective way.**
11. **Write the storyline, or plot.**
12. **Bring it to life.**

Jungle Fire™ – The Story

Here is the script we use to introduce the rules of Jungle Fire to participants through the use of video. Even though this is always the last thing to be developed (step 11), I've included it here at the outset just to give you a sense for what I was imagining when I set out to create the program.

Hello, buenos dias and welcome to the Amazon.

And welcome to my Outfitters. I've been waiting for you. I understand you've journeyed a long way here to the town of Menoas, deep in the Amazon jungle, but your journey has just begun. You are going to have a very exciting and enthralling adventure as you set out to search for the mysterious source of the dancing colors that light the morning sky. My name is Piranha Bob and I want to tell you a little bit about what I know.

Before you set off on your journey, listen while I tell you about the legend of Jungle Fire.

A long time ago, a famous explorer, Sir Rupert Thomas, came to this region looking for ancient temple ruins and the possible fortunes that he had heard of. Sir Rupert spent many days wandering along the ancient jungle paths searching out this fortune. On one particular day he emerged from the jungle dripping with perspiration, staggering, and mumbling. It is thought that he had been taken by malaria. As he fell to the ground in a state of delirium he was heard rambling on about diamonds – huge diamonds – lot's of diamonds, diamonds, diamonds, diamonds. He then fell into a state of unconsciousness. When he came to, people gathered around and said, "Tell us, tell us about these diamonds!" Sir Rupert sat up and looked around at all the people waiting anxiously to hear of these great diamonds. And then as clearly as if he had never taken ill, he said "Diamonds? I don't know what you're talking about." He denied everything.

Now, a month later, Sir Rupert began to plan another journey into the jungle. He gathered burlap bags, canoes, and other supplies along with an experienced crew of

"Sir Rupert and his crew were never to be found – no flesh, no bones. No diamonds."

guides and started back into the jungle. This time he discovered those diamonds. It was decided that to gather as many diamonds as possible he and his crew would need to set up camp. Once camp was set, it was necessary to protect himself and his crew from all the dangers of the jungle. After several hours of working in the intense heat collecting diamonds, it is believed that malaria struck again. This time Sir Rupert was not so fortunate. He and his crew were never to be found – no flesh, no bones. No diamonds.

To this day, there are still believed to be mountains and mountains of diamonds. Let me explain. When the sun rises in the morning, the rays of light strike the facets of those millions of diamonds and a rainbow of color sparkles and splashes across the morning sky. Blues and yellows, purples and pinks dance across the sky. Late in the day as the sun begins to fade, the colors fade as well and can be seen no more. Now, the villagers I've met in this region, not knowing the source nor the whereabouts of these dancing colors have given them a name. They've called them "Jungle Fire."

I can see you're excited to be here today and have come all this way because you've heard of the legend of Sir Rupert Thomas, his mysterious disappearance and, of course, "Jungle Fire." I can only hope that you are successful!

1 WHAT'S THE OBJECTIVE?

- Be precise
- Summarize the content
- Include rationale
- How long should it take?
- Decide your intention
  - Build conviction?
  - Create awareness?
  - Practice?

▼ *This shows the desired learning that participants should leave with.*

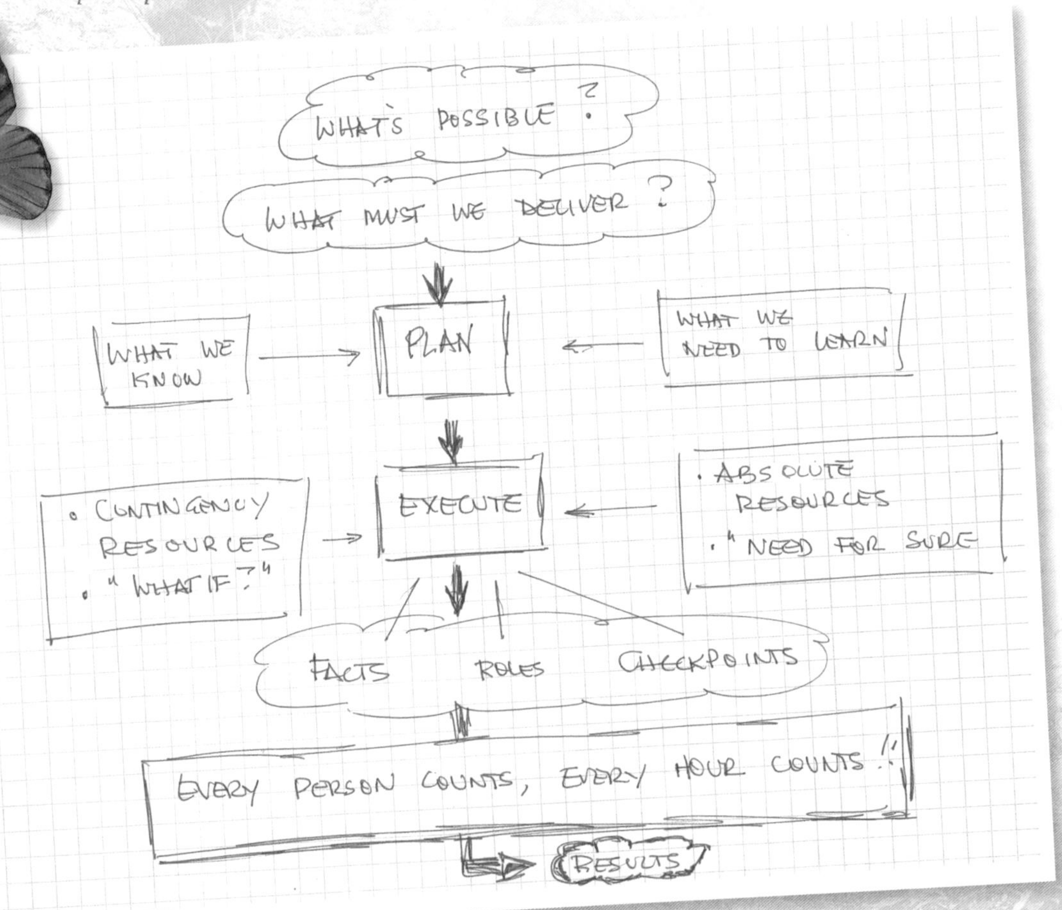

2 WHAT COMPONENTS OF THE LEARNING WILL BE IN THE EXPERIENCE?

- What do you want to teach?
- What do you **NOT** want to teach?
- Which components are major, and which are minor?
- What does successful behavior look like (i.e., how will you"win?")

In Jungle Fire, the objective is to be as productive as possible at work through:

- Strong goal orientation
- Improved planning skills
- Better use of information
- Effective use of colleagues

Some of the major components in Jungle Fire, are:

- Lots of opportunity to plan
- The importance of linking the planning to a clear goal
- How vital is relevant information to creating a great plan?
- The value of effective teamwork

3 WHAT KINDS OF ENVIRONMENTS NATURALLY LEND THEMSELVES TO THESE BEHAVIORS?

Activity

- Building
- Discovering
- Interacting
- Designing
- Adventuring

Approach

- Competition
- Collaboration
- Negotiation
- Creativity
- Execution

Pathway

- Moving from competition to collaboration
- Staying with one approach
- Series of individual discrete events
- Learning as you go (i.e., discovery)

Pace

- Measured
- Chaotic
- Fast
- Controlled
- Flexible

Design

- Learn from failure?
- Learn from success?
- When? During the experience, or at the end?

4 WHAT KIND OF THEME WILL BEST SERVE THE EXPERIENCE?

- Effective
- Novel
- Fun

5 GIVE IT A TITLE

- Short
- Has Meaning
- Punchy
- Intriguing
- Enticing

Jungle Adventure
Amazon Adventure
Jungle Warriors
Jungle Fire™

6 CREATE A ROUGH OUTLINE THAT BRINGS IT TOGETHER

- Try a few
- Elaborate, brainstorm, explore
- Sketch it out
- Tinker
- Select an approach

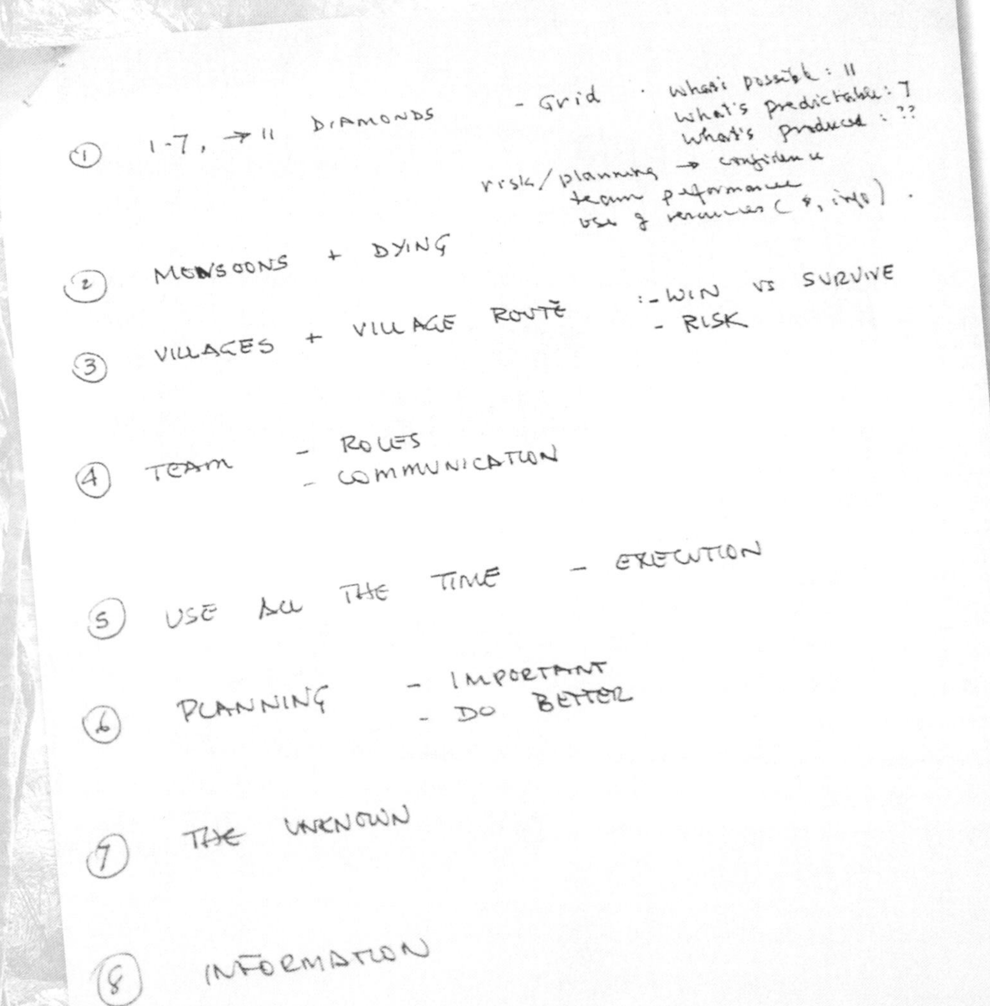

◀ *These are some components to consider including.*

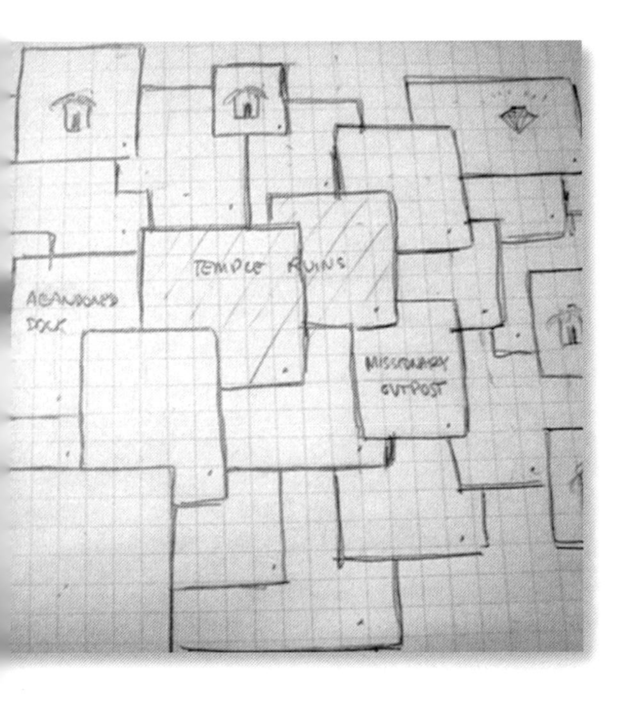

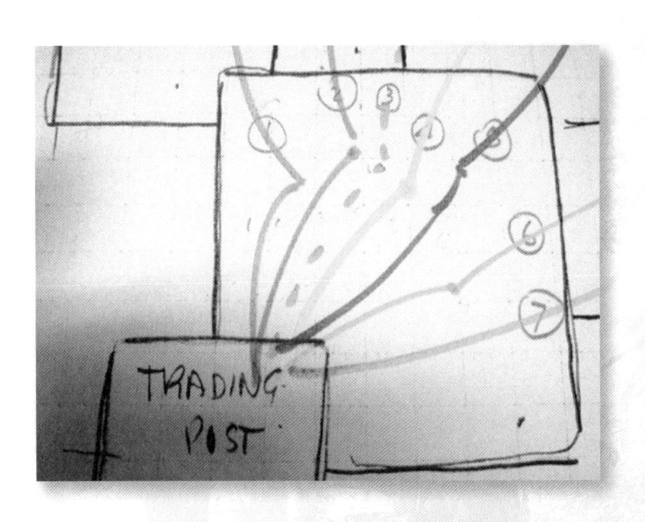

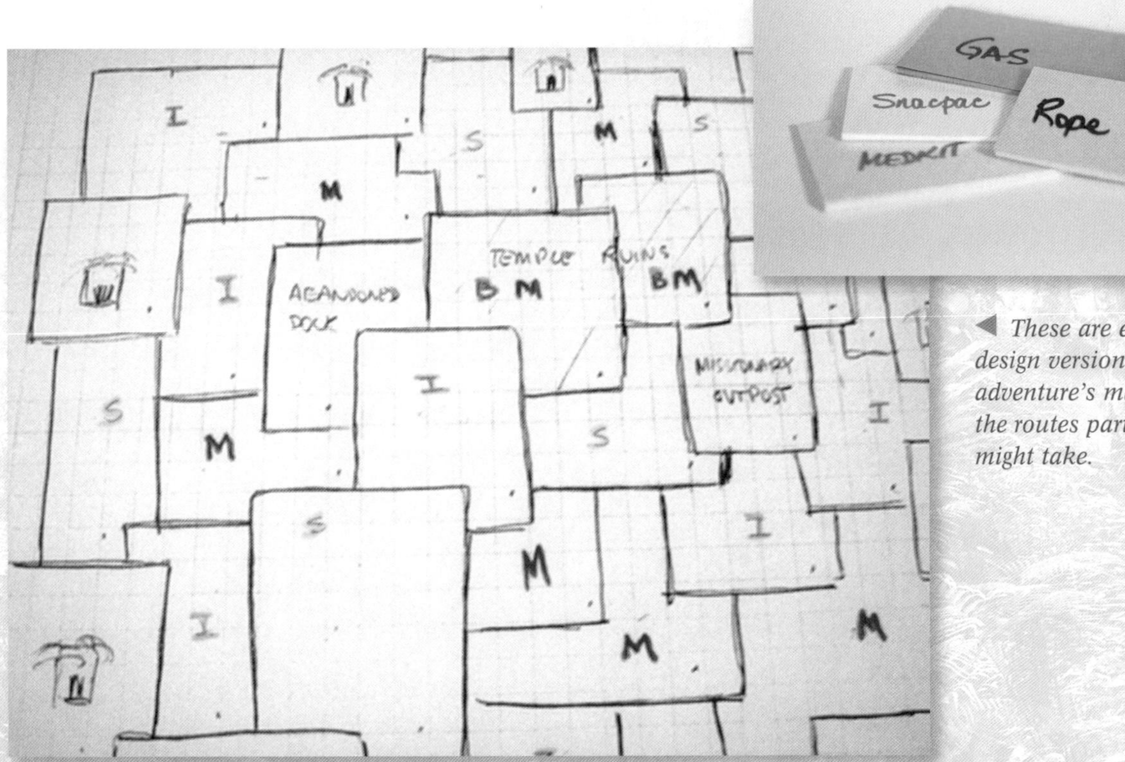

These are early design versions of the adventure's map and the routes participants might take.

7 ADD SPECIFIC DETAIL OF WHAT NEEDS TO BE TAUGHT

- What aspect will teach what?
- What needs more detail?
- What needs less detail?
- Add, or remove, complexity
- Ensure "this aspect" teaches "that outcome"
- Redesign, and rework until there is a direct (but not obvious) themed link between the experience, its activities, and the desired learning (i.e., mask the learning)
- Make notes for your debrief – how to bring the learning alive

In STEP 1, an objective of Jungle Fire™ was Improved Planning Skills, so included were:

- Up-front planning
- Choices on route, supplies, etc.
- When you can buy the supplies you'll use
- Overcoming known problems
- Charting your route
- A really clear goal

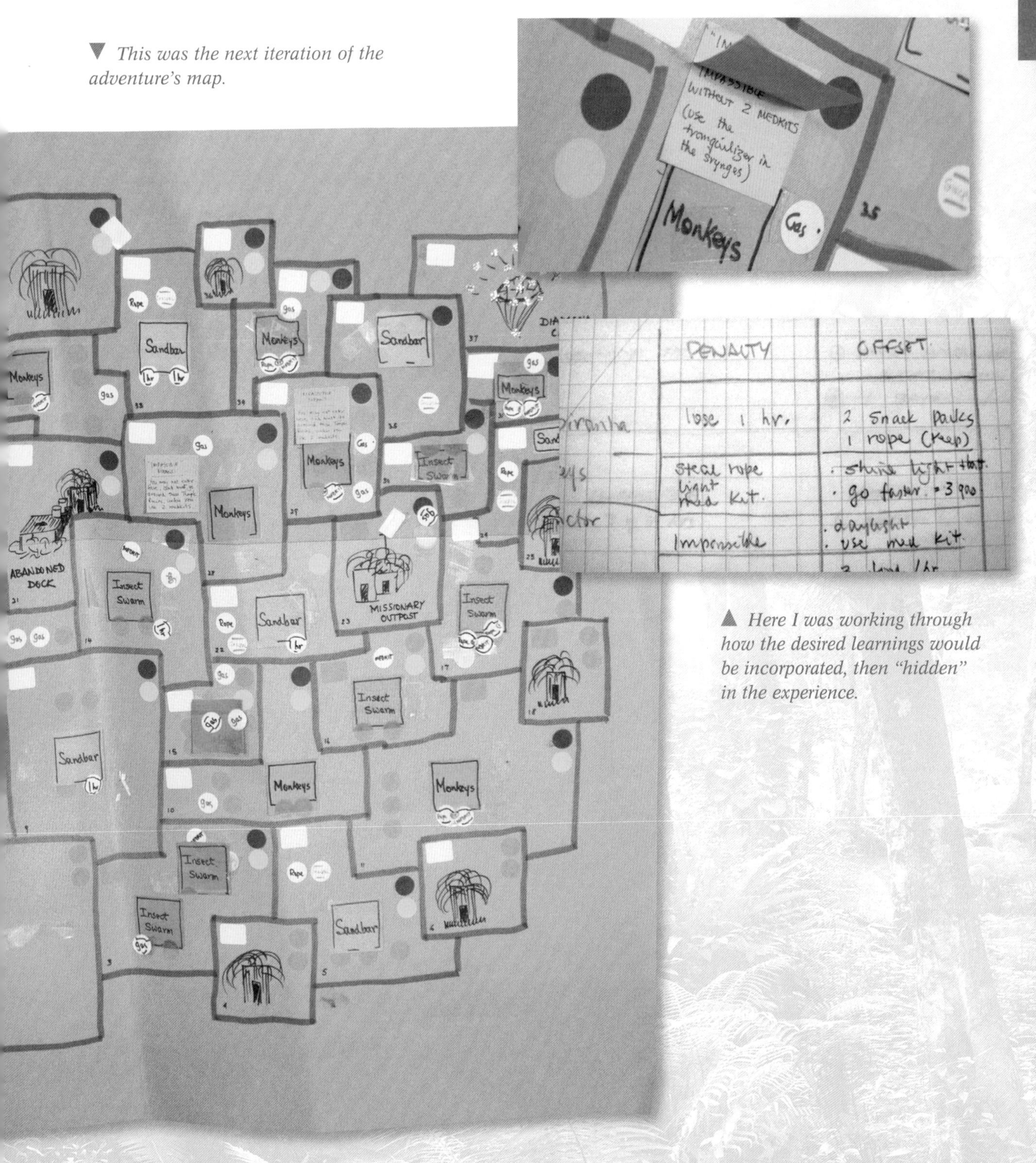

▼ *This was the next iteration of the adventure's map.*

▲ *Here I was working through how the desired learnings would be incorporated, then "hidden" in the experience.*

8 WORK OUT THE NUMBERS

- Measurable is best
- Scoring to win
- Team equity – all have an equal opportunity to win
- All can participate fully
- Use the numbers to reflect the learning

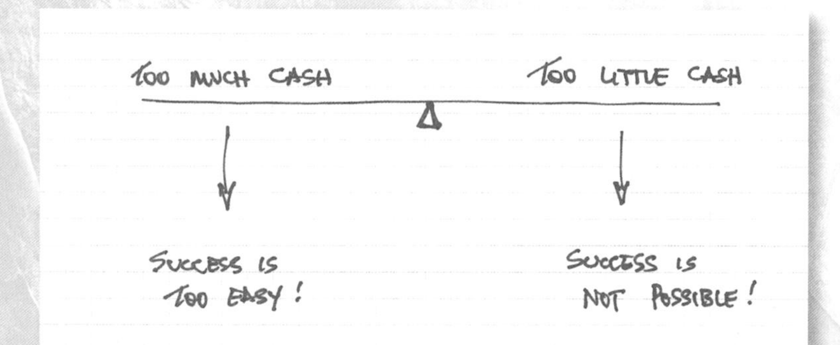

▲ *Working through the numbers is the basis of most experiences.*

9 TEST, REWORK, TEST, REWORK...

- Is there a role for everyone?
- How's the timing?
- Assess against your vision
- Does it deliver the outcomes?
- Too complex? Too easy? Too hard?
- Get input
- Expect the pendulum effect

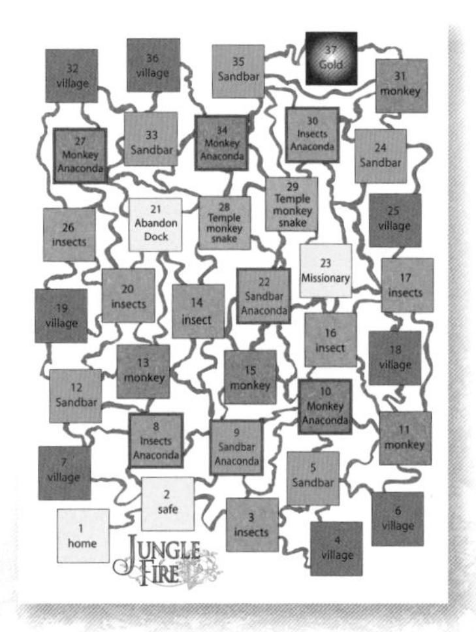

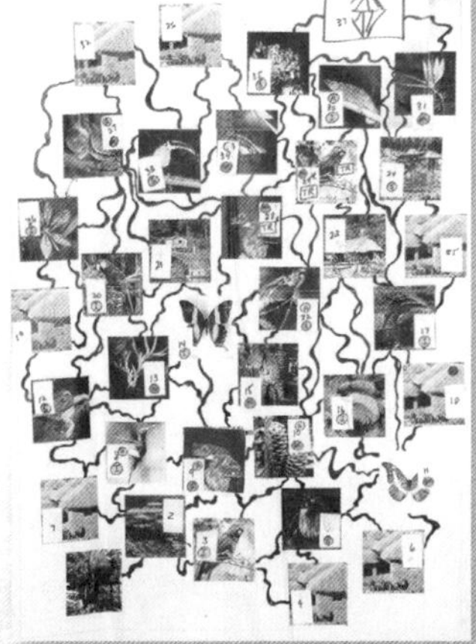

▶ *The evolution of the design of the Adventure's map.*

PIRANHA BOB'S REP

As Piranha Bob's Rep, distribute the Jungle Informati Packets your team decides to view. Piranha Bob has Jungle Information Packets available for viewing. Ea information packet take one hour to view.

...and DI

As Diamond Discover with one Diamond fo Diamond Cache.

BUSHWHACKER

As the Bushwhacker for your team you are responsible ments are placed on resource stickers from appropriate spot on

PIRANHA BOB'S BANKER

On behalf of Piranha Bob's Outfitters, sell your team resources. Piranha Bob's Outfitters has Gas, Snacpacs, Rope, Medkits and Tiger St... Your team has

RIVER LOOKOUT GUIDE

As River Lookout Guide for your team, you must each hour is properly recorded. First, label each ti sticker (1 - 24). Second, ensure each time sticker on the appropriate spot on each location card.

Keep track of your team's use of time. Watch fo spent at Piranha Bob's Outfitters and the Diam Watch for perils that eat up your team's time.

NAVIGATOR

As Navigator for your team, you are responsible for your team's money and resources. Use your team's $4500 to purchase resources from Piranha Bob's Outfitters. Trade Tiger Stones for resources with the Village Banker.

As Navigator, you are also responsible for reading the location cards and posting them on your map.

Calculate and post your team's final score on the team score wall chart.

10 PREPARE THE RULES TO BE DELIVERED IN AN ENTERTAINING AND EFFECTIVE WAY

- Tell the story, and put them in it
- Select the best medium (video, PowerPoint, facilitator dependent)
- Include humor
- Create anticipation and a desire to get going immediately
- Be clear!
- Include examples

11 WRITE THE STORYLINE OR PLOT

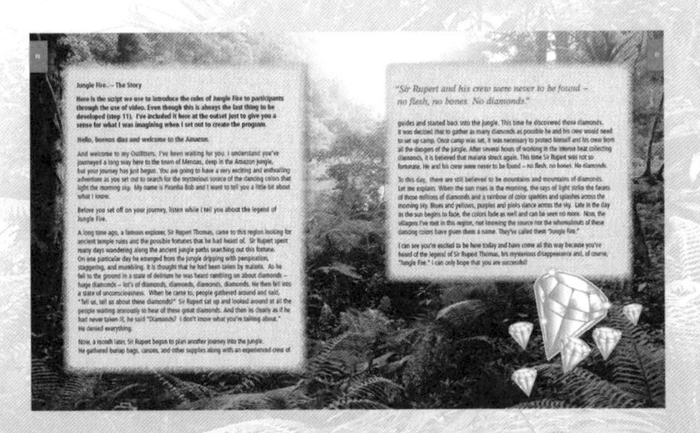

Jungle Fire – The Story

Here is the script we use to introduce the rules of Jungle Fire to participants through the use of video. Even though this is always the last thing to be developed (step 11), I've included it here at the outset just to give you a sense for what I was imagining when I set out to create the program.

Hello, bomos dias and welcome to the Amazon.

And welcome to my Outfitters. I've been waiting for you. I understand you've journeyed a long way here to the town of Menoas, deep in the Amazon jungle, but your journey has just begun. You are going to have a very exciting and enthralling adventure as you set out to search for the mysterious source of the dancing colors that light the morning sky. My name is Piranha Bob and I want to tell you a little bit about what I know.

Before you set off on your journey, listen while I tell you about the legend of Jungle Fire.

A long time ago, a famous explorer, Sir Rupert Thomas, came to this region looking for ancient temple ruins and the possible fortunes that he had heard of. Sir Rupert spent many days wandering along the ancient jungle paths searching out this fortune. On one particular day he emerged from the jungle dripping with perspiration, staggering, and mumbling. It is thought that he had been taken by malaria. As he fell to the ground in a state of delirium he was heard rambling on about diamonds – huge diamonds – lot's of diamonds, diamonds, diamonds, diamonds. He then fell into a state of unconsciousness. When he came to, people gathered around and said, "Tell us, tell us about these diamonds!" Sir Rupert sat up and looked around at all the people waiting anxiously to hear of these great diamonds. And then as clearly as if he had never taken ill, he said "Diamonds? I don't know what you're talking about." He denied everything.

Now, a month later, Sir Rupert began to plan another journey into the jungle. He gathered burlap bags, canoes, and other supplies along with an experienced crew of

"Sir Rupert and his crew were never to be found – no flesh, no bones. No diamonds."

guides and started back into the jungle. This time he discovered those diamonds. It was decided that to gather as many diamonds as possible he and his crew would need to set up camp. Once camp was set, it was necessary to protect himself and his crew from all the dangers of the jungle. After several hours of working in the intense heat collecting diamonds, it is believed that malaria struck again. This time Sir Rupert was not so fortunate. He and his crew were never to be found – no flesh, no bones. No diamonds.

To this day, there are still believed to be mountains and mountains of diamonds. Let me explain. When the sun rises in the morning, the rays of light strike the facets of those millions of diamonds and a rainbow of color sparkles and splashes across the morning sky. Blues and yellows, purples and pinks dance across the sky. Late in the day as the sun begins to fade, the colors fade as well and can be seen no more. Now, the villagers I've met in this region, not knowing the source nor the whereabouts of these dancing colors have given them a name. They've called them "Jungle Fire."

I can see you're excited to be here today and have come all this way because you've heard of the legend of Sir Rupert Thomas, his mysterious disappearance and, of course, "Jungle Fire." I can only hope that you are successful!

◀ *This was shown at the beginning of the section.*

12 BRING IT TO LIFE

- Artwork
- Sizzle
- Color
- Drama
- Detail
- Look and feel

PIRANHA BOB'S OUTFITTERS

FIFTY DOLLARS $50

TWENTY FIVE DOLLARS $25

THE ADVENTURE CONTINUES...

REUTERS/Petr Josek

The impact of being part of a powerful experiential learning event can be transformative. It can alter how we see the world, how we interact with others, and how we approach our commitments.

The learning continues long after the training. It often extends into our family or off-work activities, perhaps with charities we support, or committees we sit on. What we've discovered for ourselves in the program are principles that we make our own, usually to the benefit not only of ourselves but also those around us, and with whom we work.

In many ways the experience we went through is so "real" in our minds that it's like we were actually there in person, not just in mind. If we – as those with the very heavy responsibility for shaping the behaviors of others through training – can achieve that, then we will truly have made a difference in the lives of others!

It's my hope that this book has been and will be of some help to you on that journey.

APPENDIX

Additional Resources on Experiential Learning

1. **Experiential Learning in a Training and Development Class**
   LISA A. BURKE, University of Tennessee at Chattanooga, 2008

2. **From Experience to Experiential Learning: Cultural Intelligence as a Learning Capability for Global Leader Development**
   KOK-YEE NG, Nanyang Technological University
   LINN VAN DYNE, Michigan State University
   SOON ANG, Nanyang Technological University, 2009

3. **Experiential Learning Theory: A Dynamic, Holistic Approach to Management Learning, Education and Development**
   ALICE Y. KOLB AND DAVID A. KOLB
   Weatherhead School of Management
   Case Western Reserve University, 2008

4. **Designing Effective Learning Systems for Management Education: Student Roles...**
   CYNTHIA A LENGNICK-HALL; MARTHA M SANDERS
   Academy of Management Journal, 1997

5. **Using Simulation-Based Training to Enhance Management Education**
   EDUARDO SALAS
   JESSICA L. WILDMAN, University of Central Florida
   RONALD F. PICCOLO, Rollins College, 2009

6. **A Meta-Analytic Review of Behavior Modeling Training**
   PAUL J. TAYLOR, Chinese University of Hong Kong and University of Waikato
   DARLENE F. RUSS-EFT, Oregon State University
   DANIEL W. L. CHAN, Chinese University of Hong Kong, 2005

7. **Learning Styles and Learning Spaces: Enhancing Experiential Learning in Higher Education**
   ALICE Y. KOLB, Experience-Based Learning Systems
   DAVID A. KOLB, Case Western Reserve University, 2005

8. **A Review of Scholarship on Assessing Experiential Learning Effectiveness**
   JERRY GOSEN
   JOHN WASHBUSH
   University Wisconsin, Whitewater, 2004

9. **Does Active Learning Work? A Review of the Research**
   MICHAEL PRINCE
   Department of Chemical Engineering, Bucknell University, 2004

10. **When is PBL More Effective? A Meta-synthesis of Meta-analyses Comparing PBL to Conventional Classrooms**
    JOHANNES STROBEL AND ANGELA VAN BARNEVELD, 2009

APPENDIX

Additional Resources on Experiential Learning

11. **Completing the Experience: Debriefing in Experiential Educational Games**
    SCOTT NICHOLSON
    School of Information Studies, Syracuse University
    Systems, Cybernetics and Informatics, 2013

12. **Enhancing Deep Learning: Lessons from the Introduction of Learning Teams in Management Education in France**
    LIZ BORREDON
    SYLVIE DEFFAYET EDHEC Business School, Lille, France
    ANN C. BAKER George Mason University, Arlington, VA, USA
    DAVID KOLB Case Western Reserve University, Cleveland, OH, USA
    Journal of Management Education, 2011

13. **Experiential Learning Theory: From Theory To Practice**
    MARY MCCARTHY, Nova Southeastern University, USA
    Journal of Business & Economics Research, 2010

14. **Experiential Learning – What do we Know? A Meta-analysis of 40 Years of Research**
    GERALD (JERRY) F. BURCH, Tarleton State University
    JOHN H. BATCHELOR, University of West Florida
    NATHAN A. HELLER, Tarleton State University
    JOANNA SHAW, Tarleton State University
    WALTER KENDALL, Tarleton State University
    BEVERLY TURNER, Tarleton State University
    Developments in Business Simulation and Experiential Learning, 2014

15. **How Debriefing Strategies Can Improve Student Motivation and Self-Efficacy in Game-Based Learning**
    CIGDEM UZ BILGIN, Yildiz Technical University
    YOUNGKYUN BAEK, Boise State University
    HYUNGSUNG PARK, ShinGu University
    Journal of Educational Computing Research, 2015

16. **The effect of problem-based learning in nursing education: a meta-analysis**
    IN-SOO SHIN, Jeonju University
    JUNG-HEE KIM, Catholic University of Korea
    Advances in Health Sciences Education Theory and Practice, 2013

17. **Do team and individual debriefs enhance performance? A meta-analysis**
    TANNENBAUM S.I., CERASOLI C.P., The Group for Organizational Effectiveness, USA
    Human Factors, 2013